Who Do You Want To Be?

The Art of Presenting Yourself With Ease

Glynn Bedington

Silvercat Publications
San Diego, California

Cover by Tyler Blik Design, San Diego, California.

10 9 8 7 6 5 4 3 2 1

Library of Congress Cataloging-in-Publication Data

Bedington, Glynn, date.
    Who do you want to be the art of presenting yourself with ease.
/ by Glynn Bedington.
     p.   cm.
    ISBN 0-9624945-9-3 (pbk.)
    1. Self-actualization (Psychology) 2. Self-perception. 3. Goa
(Psychology)   I. Title.
    BF637.S4B424 1995
    158'.2--dc20   95-765
                                        CIP

Printed in the United States of America

Table of Contents

1. Introduction: Who Are You? 7

Part I: Building Blocks

2. You Are What You Think 15

3. Concentration: The Ultimate Gift 27

4. Intention And Understanding 37

5. Recreating vs. Repeating Information 47

6. How To Say What You Mean 53

7. Looking the Part 67

8. Turn Fear Into Excitement 75

9. Allow the Unique You To Emerge 83

Part II: Turning Technique Into Inspiration

10. Turning On Your Inner Voice 93

11. Getting Comfortable With Your Audience 101

12. Keeping Your Audience Satisfied 111

13. Intentions, Goals, And Personal Power 117

14. Seven Steps To Perfect Presentations 125

Part III: Some Applications

15. Preparing For An Interview 133

16. Technical Concerns For Presentations 145

17. Major Presentations 153

18. Presentation In Everyday Life 161

Special Thanks

This book was written as the result of the love and support I received from many people in my life. First, my parents for being effective teachers; second my many clients who willingly mastered these techniques. Next Bobby Stepp for planting the idea in my head; my husband Paul for providing the time, patience, and discerning ear I so often have needed; and my daughter Guyanna for putting it all into perspective. Also, my dear friends who carefully read the manuscript and gave highly constructive comments; and finally, my dedicated and patient publisher, without whom this book would have ended before it began.

Thank you all.

1

Introduction: Who Are You?

Pilgrims traveled from all corners of ancient Greece to ask the Oracle at Delphi questions about life and the future. Inscribed above the Oracle were the simple words, "Know Thyself." Of all the wisdom that the Oracle dispensed, this could have been the wisest, and it was freely available to anyone who bothered to look. Whatever the pilgrim's question, the answer began with the simple truth that the future grows out of the present. In order to get somewhere, to become someone, or to achieve something, you have to know where you are—and who you are. Only then can you begin to get a clear picture of what the future might hold.

My work as a presentation trainer has brought me into contact with hundreds of modern-day pilgrims seeking the same kinds of answers. I teach my clients skills that I have learned during my years of work on the stage, where the art of self-presentation has been developed to its finest expression. Even here, the Oracle's lesson remains as true today as it was centuries ago.

In the world of the theater, "Know Thyself" means "Know Thy Character." Actors strive to become their characters on stage, to act as if the play was real life and their characters were real people. The most powerful and convincing performances happen when the actors, at least for their time on the stage, forget the distinctions between themselves and the characters they are portraying.

In a very profound way, actors consciously apply the tools and techniques of personal growth and development. What they and my clients have come to understand is that *all* relationships begin with the relationship to the self, whether that self is a character in a play or a real person. If you hope to change yourself or to change your future, you have to begin by understanding who you are right now. Otherwise, you face the overwhelming task of trying to plot your destination when you don't know where you are starting from. Only when you know who you are can you turn your attention to becoming who you want to be.

The Importance of Intention

It is necessary to know who you are, but it is not enough. It is just as important that you have very clear intentions, not only about becoming something more, but also about who or what you want to become. With clear intentions, you can get there; with less than clear intentions, the best you can hope for is to end up somewhere.

Actors know this. In order to become their characters, they have to discover what their characters intend. It is intention, in fact, that gives the character life. What is true on the stage is true in the real world as well. Any successful presentation of self, whether on a stage before an audience or in a conference room before a client, must have a clear intention at its core.

A clear intention is nothing more or less than a decision to act in pursuit of a specific goal, a decision to set in motion the actions that lead to that desired outcome. Intention stokes the desire to carry out the necessary actions. An intention is always a positive assertion: *I want to walk straight and tall* or *I want to open people's minds* instead of *I don't want to slouch* or *I don't like prejudice.*

We'll see over and over again that intentions are the key to presentation. It is important to define your intentions clearly and keep them in plain sight. Intentions guide the actions that produce results. This is true whether you are aware of your actual intentions or not. Even when your intentions are not conscious, they still govern how you act, what you do, and how you present yourself.

Clarifying and knowing your intentions are so important that we will return to these subjects repeatedly throughout this book. For the present, however, we need to pay some attention to the unfortunate fact that unclarified and unwitting intentions rule the self-presentations of so many people.

The Honest Camera

I almost always begin the first session with a new client with the question, *Who do you want to be? How do you want others whom you are meeting for the first time to describe you?* Typically, answers are something like "She's professional, intelligent, and understanding," or "He's clear-headed, commited, and tough," or "He's understanding, perceptive, and capable."

While my clients are answering these questions, I am running the video camera. Toward the end of the first session, I usually suggest we take a look at what the camera has seen. Most clients feel uncomfortable: *Oh no!...Do I have to look at it?* Usually, I remind the clients that everyone else has already seen them the way they are and that this is their opportunity to see how they come across. For many clients, it is their first opportunity to see how they are displaying their intentions to the rest of the world.

Perhaps it is the camera's honesty that makes so many of us quiver at the thought of seeing ourselves as others see us. Perhaps it is because the camera wakes us up to what we really look, act, and sound like. Perhaps it is because the camera dramatizes the differences between where we are and where we want to be. Whatever the reason, we still need to take a look, to stand outside ourselves and see what everyone else already knows.

As my clients and I watch the video playback, a predictable response usually occurs. At first, there is an inevitable self-bashing: *Boy! Do I need a haircut...I need to replace that jacket...Am I really that fat?* Then we begin to explore the interesting and valuable pieces of information the video has to offer. We view the tape with the sound turned off—vocal expression often gets in the way of real seeing. I start by asking clients to imagine that they have never seen the person on the screen before (often they haven't) and to respond spontaneously to questions about the person on screen. *What is she talking about?...How does he feel?...Does she look comfortable?...How does he feel about the person he is talking to?*

I ask clients to answer in the third person as if they truly are describing strangers. *She looks uncomfortable with her subject....She looks completely involved....He looks so angry....She looks nervous (confident, tentative, etc.)*. Then I ask what, specifically, provoked the reaction. At first, clients may feel frustrated or tongue-tied: *I don't know; she just looks that way*. Then they often become much more observant and specific: *The shoulders—the shoulders and the chest. He has no movement there. He doesn't even seem to be alive in that area....She keeps putting her hands in front of her face; it's really distracting....Look at his head—it tilts to the right when he talks; he looks so awkward....She's clutching the arms of the chair as if she were scared to death, and look how tightly her arms and hands are clenched!*

Even if this were only a process of self-discovery, it would be helpful. But it is much more. It gives clients an opportunity to see how their intentions manifest themselves in their actions. It allows them to see how their physical presentation can contradict their verbal presentation. It shows them how they direct or misdirect the energy they have at their disposal. Finally, it permits them to take an inventory of the strengths and weaknesses that they project when they present, especially those that they might not be aware of.

Muscles Have Memories

For centuries, students of literature and the theater have known something that psychologists have discovered only during the past century: our muscles have memories. The muscles hold attitudes and reflexes that prepare them to respond to whatever is happening. The English language is full of adjectives that suggest a physical analogy. What do you picture, for example, when you hear of a *hulking* presence or a *slouching* demeanor or a *retiring* personality?

We teach our muscles to remember. Over a lifetime, we assume certain patterns of response to circumstances and events. The therapist Fritz Perls described the process of 'armoring,' in which we habitually tense our muscles as we perceive a need to protect ourselves. Fully armored, we send signals to others to *stay away*. We misplace our energy, directing too much to this part of the body or too little to that part. Or we spend an inordinate amount of energy trying to control our spontaneity, with the result that we end up appearing unexpressive and bottled up inside. The result is the same. Those to whom we are speaking get the message; they react to the armor and not to the person.

The effects of this 'muscle memory' are often pretty obvious. We communicate our hidden messages. Except they are not hidden, despite our best efforts. They are, literally, as plain as the nose on your face.

Releasing The Muscles.

We need to release these muscle-holding patterns if we want to present to our full potential. I help my clients learn to release their muscles by applying some techniques first developed by the Australian orator Mathius Alexander. I have clients sit on a stool. Because the neck is one of the most common areas in which we hold tension to excess, I focus their attention on the neck. I work my hands and fingers around the neck muscles, applying and releasing pressure while asking the clients to release the tension locked in specific areas. Then I move to the shoulders and arms, two other areas of frequent blockage, repeating the same process and the same instructions.

Releasing pent up muscle tension sometimes releases the thoughts or the memories of the real events that initially caused the pattern of tension. It is not unusual for a client to feel vulnerable or exposed when this kind of tension is released. Despite the discomfort, the experience can often help us identify precisely what is going on when the muscles tighten. This can be a freeing experience, both liberating the client from the tyranny of the past and teaching the client a new technique for dealing with the future.

Taking An Inventory

Finally, we round out this *Know Thyself* process by taking an inventory, not of the client's weaknesses, but of his strengths. What are the tools that the client can use? What does the client do well? What personal attributes can she count on? What abilities does he have? How has she already learned to make up for a perceived lack of certain talents or qualities? Usually, my clients are surprised as they begin to recognize just how many strengths, talents, and abilities they really have.

It happened to me, too. When I was a child, my playmates and I used to play a *Who Am I* game. We would stand before the group and mimic some characteristic or behavior of another to see if the group could identify whom we were portraying. Once, my best friend squinched up her face with a smile so broad that her eyes became slits. Without a moment of hesitation, the entire room screamed out my name!

I felt humiliated. Did I look like that? Was I really that ridiculous? With a face like that, I should lock myself in my room and never come out again! The sting stayed with me for days. I tried not to smile, but inevitably I'd forget. I'd smile...then I'd remember my best friend 'making fun' of my face. I'd want to die all over again.

Years later, a reviewer wrote about one of my theatrical performances, "With a face like the full moon, she lights up the stage." My face! It lit up the stage! It wasn't a curse after all, but a blessing! All this time I had been ashamed of something that was a true asset. It took me a while to see, but once I recognized this particular asset, I knew that it would be my ally for the rest of my career.

It is important to take a true inventory. Only when you know where you are and what you are carrying with you can you know where you are going and how you are going to get there. This knowledge and understanding of yourself is the basis for growth and change. You can't turn to others to make yourself a powerful presenter any more than you can blame others because you are not there yet. You can only acknowledge who you are and where you are now, change, and watch the changes reflected in your life.

The journey of a thousand miles does indeed begin with a single step. And what a journey it can be, if you keep in mind where you are today and where you are heading. Just don't forget to enjoy the scenery along the way. The second step begins with the next chapter.

Setting The Stage

Chapter 2 begins a discussion of theatrical and personal-growth techniques that enhance both presentation and self-image. These are all 'tricks' that successful stage performers have used for years to make their performances more believable to their audiences. But it is not just the audience who need to believe. You will discover that as you make your presentations more believable to others, you will also come to believe more in yourself.

It is a cliché in the theater that technique creates inspiration. It is not enough to master a skill; you have to *know* that you have mastered it. You can then put your energy into your presentation and not into worrying about how you are going to get from here to there. In part II, which begins with Chapter 10, you will learn a number of ways of drawing great inspiration out of the techniques you have already mastered.

Along the way, you will discover the truth behind another aphorism: "To Thine Own Self Be True." What distinguishes a stage performance from a real-life presentation is this: the great actor becomes the character for the duration of the performance; the great presenter *is* the presentation. You cannot separate the presentation from the presenter. To present information believably, you have to present yourself believably.

Chapter 15 begins Part III, which discusses several real-life situations in which you may be called on to employ your presentation skills. These are the kinds of situations where people feel most uncomfortable or unsure of themselves—interviews and major presentations, for example. In these chapters, you will learn some very specific tips and recommendations for coming out ahead of the game. But you don't need to face a crisis to make use of your presentation skills. As Chapter 18 will remind you, presentation is an act of daily life. The better able you are to present yourself and what you have to offer, the easier and more rewarding your life will become.

So…turn the page and take that next step.

2

You Are What You Think

Are you your own best friend? Do you use your intimate relationship with yourself to your best advantage? Or do you, like so many people, continually criticize your weaknesses with an endless stream of negative judgments?

How you talk to yourself and how you think about yourself says a lot about your self-relationship. You communicate with yourself by means of your continual mental comments—you may even talk to yourself out loud—far more often than you talk to others. You are able to influence your own mind in ways that no one else can. When your influence is reinforced by your emotions, the intensity is even greater.

When Ginny was first beginning to understand this concept, she had an experience that taught her, in just a few seconds, to respect her own self-influence and never to ignore her power again. She had a snappy little red sports car that she was very proud of. She had wanted a red convertible since she was sixteen, and finally, at age thirty-two, her dream had become a reality. Driving the ten miles to her office each morning was a joy.

Ginny liked to drive to work with her morning coffee in hand. Everytime she set the cup on the dashboard, she knew that she was taking a risk, but she didn't care. She continued to sip her coffee and curve along the bay before meeting up with the freeway and zipping into town.

One day, wanting to make a good impression on a new client, Ginny put on a new pair of silk pants. On this particular day, her car found a curve it wasn't able to handle well and the coffee ended up on her lap. Even before she could respond consciously to her predicament, she began to hear, as if from another source, a verbal lashing that told her exactly what a jerk she was. *Oh that's just great! You knew you would spill this coffee one day. You are so stupid. You always do stupid things like this. You always ruin your good clothes. You can't take care of anything. You don't deserve to have good things.*

Near the end of her monologue, Ginny finally heard what she was saying to herself and felt what her words were doing. At once, she understood the power she had over herself. She finally realized the power of self- talk.

This came as a complete shock. Ginny had always thought she was a friend to herself, but here she was, belittling herself, apparently for no one's benefit. She became aware that until she could truly accept herself, forgiving herself for the mistakes she would easily forgive others—until she could honestly make friends with herself—she would not be able to give herself permission to fulfill her hopes and desires.

Psychologists have field days with all the reasons we relate to ourselves negatively. Many of their theories are useful tools for helping us change our self-relationships. One of these is that it is important for us to become aware of what we are doing to ourselves. We can analyze our destructive habits later. For now, the realization makes change and progress possible. Once we can see the negative relationships we have with ourselves, those relationships which seem always to be waiting in ambush for times of stress, we can make a choice. We can choose to accept that being our own worst enemy is an indelible part of our upbringings, our businesses, our finances, or our fates. Or, we can decide that the relationship is not supporting the way we want to live and that it is time for a change. For the vast majority of my clients, there really is no choice. It is time to change.

Ginny's experience in her little red sports car allowed her, for the first time, to see her self-relationship clearly. She didn't really know herself very well. She really didn't "always do stupid things" or "ruin everything she had." In fact, she was pretty good at a lot of things. And she needed to recognize that.

As a result, Ginny began to become reacquainted with herself. I urged her to tell herself who she really was and to self-talk honestly about her strengths and the areas where she wanted to improve. She enlisted her own support. She made a conscious and consistent attempt to speak to herself the way she would like to be spoken to by others. When she started expressing the old judgments, I told her to hear herself, apologize, and then restate the comments using constructive language. She began telling herself what she wanted instead of what she didn't want. "Look at the map and follow the directions carefully" is a lot more constructive than "Don't get lost like you usually do."

Ginny began to respect herself in an entirely new way. The more she practiced effective communication with herself, the easier it became. Positive changes began to occur. First, she felt more relaxed. Her anger had taken a lot of energy to maintain. She developed more tolerance for others. As she learned to care about and for herself, she began to care about and for others. She started liking what she saw when she looked in the mirror. She saw fewer faults and more strengths. She became selective about the people she spent time with and began to feel comfortable in the presence of people who felt good about themselves.

Self Talk

To understand how dynamic self-talk can be, consider the computer. Whatever you type and save will be there, unchanged, whenever you want to see it. If you save misspelled words, they will be just as misspelled when you retrieve them. The computer makes no judgement about the words; it simply saves everything. In this respect, it is very much like our subconscious minds that contain the programs of our self-talk. *Garbage in, garbage out...Clarity in, clarity out.*

A computer remembers the characters and spaces it is told to remember. The subconscious remembers the thoughts and images it is told to remember. Give it an image and place the image it memory with words tied to emotion. When Ginny said, "You knew you would spill this coffee. You always do stupid things," her subconscious remembered "spill the coffee" and "do stupid things." These were the images attached to the words she used. The emotions cemented the image in her memory. When you ask the computer for a printout of what is stored, you get a hard copy of exactly what the computer remembers. When you want a printout of what your subconscious knows, you get a set of thoughts, feelings, and ideas that become actual blueprints for action, commands to spill the coffee or to do stupid things.

Self-talk is also like a stage director. A good director can give a sense of direction to a play. So can a bad one. I was once cast in a play with a new director who hadn't quite figured out what she wanted to accomplish with the production. Consequently, she could not tell us what she wanted. She could only tell us what she *didn't* want. Her directions suffered. Rehearsals became confusing. We tried to figure out what she wanted from what she said she didn't want. It became a very frustrating guessing game for everyone.

One day, the cast decided to talk about it. We analyzed the life of the play without regard for the director's tentative guidance. We talked about what each of our characters was supposed to achieve during the play and the obstacles that each character had to overcome. We considered how one character's goals might be in conflict with those of another character. We discussed what each character would do to achieve his or her goals. One thing we never discussed was what we *wouldn't* do. We transformed a meaningless production into one that had clear focus. The director, who had not taken part in our discussions, said she didn't know the play had so much to say.

Lessons in self-talk can come from every direction. Several friends and I were once quietly discussing men. In particular, we were talking about Lynn's latest relationship, one that was going nowhere. One woman asked her, "What kind of man do you want to be with?" She didn't know. Lynn was much more certain of the kind of man she didn't want to be with—she could describe that man clearly because she had dated him so many times. But she had never taken the time to consider the qualities that she thought a man *should* have. She had just assumed that the right person would simply show up.

I suggested that she spend a little time seeking a direction, exploring her feelings and intentions in order to identify the qualities she was looking for. Then I suggested that she write a story about the kind of life she intended to have with her ideal mate. She wrote about the way they felt when they were together, the kinds of activities they enjoyed, the outlooks on life that they would share. Five months after writing that story she met the man who would, in another seven months, become her husband. This man was exactly like the man described in her story. Would she have met him anyway? Maybe. Would she have been as sure that he was the right one? Probably not.

Be careful what you ask for. You may get it. When Ginny said, "You knew you would spill that coffee," she was actually asking for what she wanted. The act of spilling it was simply a printout from her subconscious hard disk. When we actors made our decisions about our characters' intentions and obstacles, we were asking for the play to take a constructive direction. When Lynn listed the qualities she wanted in a mate, she was asking to meet someone who embodied those qualities. In each case, *asking* was the first step toward *achieving*. A clear intention helps you know what to ask for.

Our Thoughts Speak Louder Than Our Words

When I work with clients, one of my first tasks is to help them see how their self-thoughts are reflected in the way they appear to others. Once they have seen that, they can turn the process around by learning to use clear, intention-oriented thoughts. The results are often dramatic. What follows is a fictionalized exchange based on hundreds of actual dialogues with many different clients.

When you are preparing for a presentation, what do you tell yourself?

Oh, usually, "don't screw up."

What would be the opposite of 'screwing up'?

Let's see. I never thought about it before. I suppose it would be "do a good job."

And how would you know if you did a good job? What are the qualities of a good job?

I would have the audience listening to me and asking me questions afterward. I'd get business from the presentation.

So you want the audience to be involved with your presentation?

Yes.

And you want your audience to be interested in you and your product?

Yes.

And you want your audience to trust you enough to spend their hard-earned money with you?

Yes.

So the three things you want from your presentation are involvement, interest, and trust?

Yes.

Anything else?

Yes. I want to feel comfortable speaking to them.

Well that's the key isn't it. Unless you are comfortable with yourself, you can't be comfortable with others, especially when being with others requires you to persuade them to your way of thinking.

I see what you mean.

I am going to suggest that you try something.

What's that?

Give yourself a conscious command for action prior to speaking. Replace, "don't screw up" with "I am comfortable being involved with my audience. I am interested in them and therefore they are interested in me. They trust me to fulfill their needs."

Okay.

You don't look convinced.

Well, no. I'm not comfortable so why should I tell myself I am? I'm not sure they are interested in me.

Do you trust your product?

Sure. It's the best on the market.

Can you say that to your audience?

Yes, and I do.

Do you know everything you need to know about your product?

I can tell you more about my product than you'd ever want to know.

So your audience can trust you when it comes to your knowledge of the product?

Without a doubt.

Are you comfortable in letting your audience trust your knowledge of the product?

Absolutely.

Tell me. What was it that first got you interested in this product?

The guy who invented it. He thinks just like I do. He came up with a way to solve this problem and I thought that was just great.

Do you think that would be interesting to other people?

Sure.

Do you think that by sharing your interest in the inventor that you might be able to create interest from your audience?

I might. It would be worth a try.

Would you feel comfortable creating interest in something that you are interested in?

Yes, I would.

Now can you give yourself the command I suggested?

What was it again?

I am comfortable being involved with my audience. I am interested in them and therefore they are interested in me. They trust me to fulfill their needs.

That's funny. It doesn't sound so strange now. Yes, I could say it.

Can you say it with the assurance that you can achieve what it implies.

I think so.

You still don't sound convinced.

It's this audience business. I'm not a presenter. I don't feel comfortable in front of a bunch of people. I get really uncomfortable. It's just not me.

Do you ever entertain people at your house?

Sure. We have lots of friends and we have a party every couple of months.

What do you do at your parties?

Well, it depends. In the summer we have a barbecue. Sometimes we play ball afterwards. In the winter we build a big fire and just let things take care of themselves.

Have you ever had your friends watch while you barbecued or built your fire?

Sure.

Did that make you feel self-conscious?

No.

So, you felt comfortable with your friends, confident in your barbecue skills and in the 'performance' you were giving?

I see what you mean.

Would you believe me if I told you that you can transfer the confidence you have about barbecuing to speaking before a group about your product?

What do you mean?

Before you barbeque, what do you tell yourself?

Gee, I never think about it. I probably just remember the last time I barbecued and do it the same way.

And the last time was successful?

Sure, If there's one thing I'm good at, it's a barbeque.

So you give yourself an unconscious command based on success?

Yes.

What is your unconscious command for public speaking based on?

Failure, being uncomfortable, feeling stupid and boring.

Do you see the difference?

Yes. It seems so obvious.

So...How are you going to change it?

Change the command.

To what?

I am comfortable being involved with my audience. I am interested in them and therefore they are interested in me. They trust me to fulfill their needs.

How do you feel when you say that?

Okay! I'm starting to see what you mean. I'll give it a try tomorrow!

Who Do You Think You Are?

Thoughts have power. In many ways, the difference between a person who is successful and powerful and one who is wondering what it takes to make it is self-image and self-talk. Everyone engages in self-chatter. The successful person, however, is likely to spend much less time making or listening to negative self-judgments and much more time using self-talk to his or her advantage.

If you find that your self-judgments are getting in your way, spend some time looking at your self-talk. Is it helping you? Is it contributing to your success or your happiness? Or are you undermining your efforts and your self-image?

Pay attention to your negative self-talk. Most of the time, it is just some stale old tape you've been playing for too long. Look at what you are saying. If you take an inventory of your life and accomplishments, you will almost certainly find that your self-talk is badly in error. The best way to shut the self-talk up is to let your successes talk louder.

Take note of the feelings you associate with your successes. These feelings can become valuable tools. Identify a word or an image that helps you remember these feelings. Practice the art of recalling the feeling by recalling the word or idea. Every time you need a lift or a little positive self-encouragement, remember the words or feelings and let them help you get back in control of yourself and your presentation.

3

Concentration: The Ultimate Gift

In communication, concentration is the ultimate gift. Not just any old concentration, but effective, focused concentration. The goal of all communication is for the receiver to receive as much as the giver gives. Effective, focused concentration makes this give-and-take much easier to achieve.

Learning To Concentrate

We all know how to concentrate. You wouldn't be able to get out of bed each morning if you didn't. However, maintaining concentration when you are the focus of someone else's attention is a different task. Imagine that you suddenly learned that every move you made from the time you woke up to the time you left the house was closely observed and scrutinized by someone other than yourself. You would probably be too self-conscious to accomplish even the simple activities of starting out the day.

This is one of the things that happens when most people speak before a group. They become aware that 50, 100, 1,000 or more eyes are looking back at them.

The speaker stands; the audience sit. The speaker speaks; the audience listen. The speaker is bathed in light; the audience sit in relative darkness. The speaker has a microphone which amplifies every sound. The speaker sees people arrive late and leave early, people fall asleep and talk to their neighbor. The speaker hears sounds from adjoining rooms. The speaker hears a constant dialogue of self-thoughts and self-judgments about the speech. And, oh yes, the speaker also has to deliver the message the audience came to hear.

Actors learn early in their training that self-consciousness impedes concentration. Actors learn to change the focus of their concentration at will. To train actors in this skill, many theater teachers use the following exercise.

A student, Charles, is asked to stand before the class, who are instructed to look at the standing student silently but continuously. Charles has nothing to do but simply stand there. It doesn't take long before he shows signs of nervousness, discomfort, and self-consciousness. When these signs become obvious to all, the teacher tells Charles to remain standing but to focus on an activity, such as "count backwards silently from 100," or "count the tiles in the ceiling," or "draw a picture in your mind."

As soon as Charles changes his focus from himself to the activity, the class can virtually watch his tension and self-consciousness disappear. Both before and after this turning point, he is concentrating. At first, he concentrates on himself and how he feels standing in front of others with nothing to do. Then, by focussing on an activity, he gives his mind something else to concentrate on. By turning his focus from himself to the activity, Charles overcomes his self-consciousness.

Recall the discussion of self-talk in Chapter 2. Self-talk is one important way in which we focus our concentration on the image we intend to present. We direct our concentration and keep the image present in our awareness. It isn't enough to say, "just concentrate." Instead, we need to tell our mind exactly what we want to concentrate on. Then, we need to use our powers of concentration to keep our minds on target.

Concentration And Communication

Whether you are addressing a group or sharing thoughts with one other person, concentration—mental focus—is crucial. We may all know how to concentrate, but we don't always choose carefully and specifically what to concentrate on. Often, we mistakenly believe that we can concentrate on several things at once; that as long as our bodies are physically present, we can allow our minds to wander; that as long as words keep coming out of our mouths, our minds can solve other problems.

We often deceive ourselves. In reality, we cannot communicate the way we want to if we are not paying attention to the communication that is happening right now. The very way we speak our words and the very way we use our bodies tell our audience as much about what our minds are concentrating on as our words do. And, through our actions and behaviors, we tell our audience what we want them to concentrate on as well.

Exercise: To Present, Be Present

We are present when we acknowledge what our senses are telling us. This exercise will help you become accustomed to listening to your senses. Take notes as you proceed. We will come back to this exercise later.

Look around you and state out loud what you see. *I see the green leafy foliage of many trees. I see a black path curving under the leaves. I see dark shadows under the trees.* How does what you see affect you?

Close your eyes and state out loud what you hear. *I hear a car moving behind me, a truck backing up, an airplane moving over me, a bird, two birds, children calling to each other.* How does what you hear affect you?

Close your eyes and state out loud your physical sensations. *I feel the pressure of my scarf on my neck, the softness of the silk pants on my leg as I move, the tightness of my shoe on my sore toe, the stiffness in my neck, the ring on my finger.* How does what you feel affect you?

Place several edible things in front of you—a glass of water, a cup of coffee, salt, a piece of candy, for example. Close your eyes as you taste each one and state out loud what you taste. *I taste the bitterness of the coffee and feel it crawl across my tongue, the sweetness of the water, the salt mixing with my saliva.* How does what you taste affect you?

Close your eyes and state out loud what you smell. *The air smells dry and warm, I smell a faint whiff of smoke.* How does what you smell affect you?

Now consider the entire process. Look for common denominators and the things you felt most comfortable and uncomfortable with. Through your senses comes information that you cannot get through rational processes. If nothing else, your senses can teach you the secret wisdom that mystics have been preaching for years: *Be Here Now.* Every presentation you make takes place in the here and now, not in the there and then. Sharpened senses heighten the present in your presentation.

When you speak with your full attention on the images and concepts you are describing, everyone in the audience becomes attuned to your message. In fact, by paying full attention to your message, you automatically focus the audience's attention on your message. You help them listen to you. Because they hear you more nearly completely, they understand your message more nearly completely. Because they understand more of your message, they have more of an opportunity to be moved by it and to form opinions.

Concentration And Listening

Concentration, incidentally, is not just something a speaker has to be concerned with. Listeners, too, need to focus their concentration. While the speaker is concentrating on what to say, the members of the audience are fighting off the distractions of the day. Their minds wander to their desks and the piles of work they need to complete before the end of the day. They overhear conversations from the rows in front or coughing from the rows behind. They remember phone calls they need to make and jot notes to themselves. Their minds wander to the coffee and Danish they had for breakfast or the pressure building on their bladders. And while all this is going on, they are trying to listen to the speech the speaker came to give.

Now imagine you are in the audience. While you are listening, you get information from the way the speakers speak, the way they gesture, the way they pause before one word and race through the next. You learn something when they laugh gently after saying something or cough when they say something else. But you can only notice these nuances when you, too, concentrate fully while you listen.

The very act of listening enhances communication. When, as a listener, I fully concentrate on the person who is speaking to me, I am communicating my attention and encouraging the speaker to give a more complete message than he or she might have delivered otherwise. Concentrating while listening encourages openness on the part the person who is speaking.

This may seem obvious. Why, then, does the simple act of concentrating on what someone is saying give us so much trouble? For many of us the answer is simple: listening can never be passive. We need to expend energy to concentrate, and we must be willing to act on the information we receive.

Exercise: Focussed Listening

To get a feel for how much energy it takes to concentrate while listening, do this simple exercise. The next time you listen to another person, mirror the speaker's words as they are spoken by letting the words sound in your mind as if you were speaking them. Notice how much more meaning the words have than if you were listening passively.

What happens is this: your subconscious mind is responding as if you were speaking. You may even begin to perceive some of the unspoken meanings behind the words, some of the emotions, the unexpressed thoughts, the fears, and the prejudices of the speaker. The more you can concentrate on what you are hearing, the more these 'hidden' keys to understanding begin to stand out.

In Through the Senses, Out Through the Senses

We take in all of our information through our senses. Sight, hearing, feeling, taste and smell are media which allow us to learn and to experience. It is just as important for us to employ the senses when we present information. In acting terminology, this is called *Sense Memory* and *Emotional Recall*. Our goal should be to involve the whole of our being when we communicate.

Sense Memory and Emotional Recall techniques ask the actor to visit past images, emotions, or reactions and allow the senses to 'remember' the moods and emotions as fully as the experience. If you can recall being ten years old and visiting your grandmother's whenever you smell fresh-baked cookies, you are using these techniques. The smell of freshly baked cookies is a trigger which stimulates your recall of past images. If you can remember that smell when it doesn't really exist, then you may find other images and memories of grandma's house appearing at the same time.

It is obvious why this skill isan important theatrical skill—the actor has to create a three-dimensional character on stage. But Sense Memory and Emotional Recall are just as important to a communicator. When you fill your mind with an image—say, grandma's house—your emotions support that image, and the feelings you have for grandma's house come to the surface. They become 'real.' Before you can create an atmosphere for your audience, you must first create it for yourself. When you speak from that experience, you open the door for your audience to step in and experience its reality for themselves.

The key to mastering this skill is to learn how to involve your senses and your emotions in your words so you can create a complete experience for your audience to share in. This is not a difficult skill to master. Take a few minutes to review your notes from the exercise *To Present, Be Present*. As you read them over, recall the images, sounds, tastes, smells, and sensations in the same way as you originally experienced them. Hear the sounds, see the sights, taste the tastes, smell the smells, and feel the feelings. Recreate the experience. The closer you get to 'deja vu all over again,' the better you will be able to link your communication with its true emotional meaning.

"Wait a minute," you may object. "Emotional? What I talk about is dry and unemotional. I speak about facts and figures, not emotions." That may be true, but you still relate through your emotions to whatever you are presenting.

All words and ideas are connected to our senses and ultimately to our feelings and emotions. We have feelings and emotions about everything. This doesn't mean that communication needs to be emotional. But it does mean that whenever we are presenting information, even dry, objective, quantitative information, we are emotionally connected to what we are saying. If we do not pay attention to our emotional attachment to our words, we may lose control of the emotional messages we are sending. Unwanted or inappropriate attitudes may present themselves unless we pay attention to our emotional intentions. The way to make sure that your audience concentrates on what you want them to is for you to put some emotional concentration on what you are saying.

Intention And Concentration: An Example

Many of us have fears that become overwhelming when we speak before an audience. There is no end to the disgrace we can heap on ourselves simply by imagining an embarrassing presentation. Just the thought that something might go wrong while everyone is watching can make an otherwise confident adult look forward to oral surgery.

Several years ago, I watched a brilliant performance where an actor mirrored these fears so authentically that it unsettled the entire audience. The performance did this because the actor consummately understood the connections between presentation and emotions.

The second act of Geoff Hoyal's one-man production of *The Fool's Show* began with the house lights on and the stage lights off. A solitary figure was on stage: Hoyal, portraying a museum curator who was saddled with the unsettling job of asking the audience for donations.

This curator was a middle aged man who was clearly uncomfortable with his task. As he spoke, his right hand absentmindedly squirmed in search of something, anything, to touch, to hold on to, for security. It wandered, seemingly with a mind of its own, first to the cowlick at the top of his head and then to find its mate behind the man's back. The restless hand finally discovered the collection of pens in the man's plastic-lined breast pocket.

Suddenly, with great surprise, the curator became aware of his hand's activity. He was visibly horrified to find his hand grasping the wad of pens. Nervous and embarrassed, he became distressingly conscious of his pen-laden hand and his empty pocket. The simple, practical, and graceful way to handle the situation would have been for him to shift his concentration momentarily to the pens, put them back in his pocket, and then turn his attention back to his message and audience. But that is not what he did. The curator tried to divide his concentration between putting the pens back in his pocket and continuing his presentation, but it was hopeless. He couldn't concentrate on his speech, while the audience could only concentrate on his clumsy dance with the pens.

Many in the audience were touched so profoundly by Hoyal's performance that they became uncomfortable and unable to see the humor. This immensely successful performance succeeded in holding a mirror up for the audience to look into. The audience looked and really felt the curator's personal agony. They felt his embarrassment, pain, and humiliation, because each audience member saw himself on that stage.

Geoff Hoyal knew that his audience would be drawn to whatever he concentrated on, that intention begot attention. By manipulating his concentration and focus, he forced the audience to relate intimately to his character. The audience saw itself in the poor man's desperate rush to finish his speech, leave the humiliation behind, and return to the anonymity of his curator's world.

We can all learn from Hoyal's performance. Concentration is more than just following a formula or remembering a series of instructions. It is an involvement in the process, one which turns a spectator into a participant. And it is an art that can be learned, a skill that we can all use to bring our presentations to life.

4

Intention And Understanding

Theatre derives its stories from dramatic situations. These dramatic situations can be portrayed seriously or they can be turned into comedy. In either case, the plot generally involves the lack of communication between two or more characters. The audience laughs and cries as these characters create significant difficulties for themselves because of misunderstandings, lies that backfire, or information told to the wrong person. Such misadventures create the conflict that is the fabric of theatre. Actors search for conflict as part of character development. They ask: *Where is the conflict?...Is there more than one conflict?...Is the conflict obvious or hidden or somewhere in between?*

Conflict in real life situations is just as common, for much the same reason. Often, conflict in real life is clear, because all participants have definite points of view which they may or may not share with everyone involved. At other times, communication breaks down, even when everyone makes the effort to be understood. Most of the time, however, conflict is much more subtle. Generally, it happens because one or the other person misunderstands the *intent* of the communication.

When intention is unclear, confusion reigns. To avoid confusion, you need to pay clear and specific attention to your own intentions. For an everyday example of what happens when people don't pay attention, consider what happened to Robert and Bonnie.

Robert was a friendly young man who discovered his growing attraction to Bonnie, an intelligent young woman he'd known for all of his eighteen years. They had shared secrets as friends and were never concerned about, or even aware of, any sexual tension between them. Teenage hormones, however, were changing them both. When Bonnie became interested in a football player who was clearly less concerned about schoolwork than she was, Robert became jealous. He was hurt and angry that his friend was attracted to someone he considered to be beneath her.

One day as Robert walked Bonnie to class, she poured her heart out to him about her disappointment that her affections had not been returned by the football player. "I'm so confused. He used to tease me—you know, giving me a hard time about being smart and stuff. Then he asked me out so I could help him study for the exam last week. It went really well. He passed the test and I was sure he liked me. Now he won't even talk to me."

Robert put his arm around his friend and held her while Bonnie rested her head against his shoulder. Half romantically she told him, "Thanks for caring. You're really a friend. Why can't he be more like you?"

At that moment, the football player appeared. His eyes were on another young woman. In a spontaneous gesture of protection, competition, and just a bit of jealousy, Robert tried to save his friend from her misplaced affections. He steered her into a wall of lockers and threw himself at her in an awkward display of affection. The football player walked by without even noticing.

"Are you crazy?" Bonnie yelled as she pushed Robert away, trying desperately to catch the football player's attention. "I thought you were my friend!"

Robert couldn't explain his actions. He knew he'd made a mess of things when he was just trying to help. He knew Mr. Football was only using his friend to pass the exam. He thought, maybe, he could make him jealous. In any case, he thought Bonnie was smarter than to fall for Mr. Football's rather transparent tactics. This must be what his father meant when he said, "Women! You'll never understand them."

Bonnie felt hurt. She thought that she knew Robert, that he was her friend. She had always been relaxed and open with him, sharing with him her deepest feelings and secrets. Now she felt abused and vulnerable. Why did he have to act like such a...*man?* Her mother was right: "You just can't trust the bums."

Lack of clear intentions placed these two young people at odds with themselves and each other. They now had a series of conflicts to resolve, both individually and in their relationship. If their situation had been written as a television program, the conflict could have become high drama of date rape. Or, it could have become a situation comedy in which the two friends reaffirmed their warm connection after they wiped the pie off their faces. But this was the real world, where Roberts and Bonnies had to accept their own responsibilities for conflict. If they were ever going to patch things up, they would have to be willing to share their concerns and negotiate a new way of communicating.

What our couple would have seen is that each sent unclear messages of personal intention to the other. They needed to understand how their own actions, words, and erroneous beliefs contributed to the confusion. Bonnie, for instance, believed that men couldn't be trusted. Her contribution to the misunderstanding simply confirmed her original point of view. If she failed to take responsibility for her part in the miscommunication, she would continue to find herself in situations that confirmed her beliefs. To break this pattern, she needed to look at what happened and ask if her belief truly applied in this case.

Robert, for his part, needed to acknowledge his change of feelings for Bonnie. He had to understand his feelings and decide what the change meant to their relationship. He had to discover if it really was Bonnie whom he didn't understand, or if it was himself.

Clarifying Intentions

Our ability to communicate effectively with each other is largely a function of our ability to identify and act upon our clear personal intentions. Communicating clearly with ourselves requires that we know what we want for ourselves. Our intention is our clearest expression of what we want to achieve.

This might be sufficient if we were talking only to ourselves. However, we don't communicate in a vacuum. It its just as necessary to understand as much as possible about the intentions of our communication partner. The clearer we are about our own intention and the more we know about the person with whom we are communicating, the more successfully we can communicate.

How much can we really know about the person we are communicating with? Not everything, obviously. But you will be surprised by the amount that you really can know. Several things are important to bear in mind.

First, we all have our own, unique maps of reality that we have developed as a result of our upbringings and our experiences. These maps, or belief systems, direct our responses to people and situations in very personal ways. As we get to know others, we learn through their words and actions something about their maps of reality. The more we know another, the better able we are both to understand that person's map of reality and to predict something about their behavior. The more we allow another to understand our map of reality, the better able we are to meet where we both are comfortable.

Second, we each have our own sets of needs and wants. These often serve as blinders on our attention. Unless we are able to address these desires to the satisfaction of our communication partner (and vice versa), our attentions may be focussed on different things. Communication may suffer because we may not be saying what our partner wants to hear and the partner may be talking about something different from what we think we are talking about. Communication is much more likely to succeed when everyone's wants and needs are acknowledged. Whether we are assessing the needs of a stranger or considering what we already know about an old friend, understanding the needs and wants of the person we are talking to is very important.

Normally, an individual's wants and needs interact with the individual's map of reality to produce a unique communications package. The fuller the picture you have of this package, the better able you will be to make your point so that your partner is able to respond. This picture does not have to be fuzzy, even when you are dealing with a stranger. There are a number of steps you can take to bring it into focus so you can use it to guide your actions.

Clarify your own intentions: What is it that you want to get out of this encounter? If you don't know, you run the risk of getting something you wouldn't have wanted in the first place.

Observe and listen: Pay attention to what your partner says and does. This is your major source of information about what the other's needs are right now. Give it your full attention, as you learned to do in Chapter 3.

Analyze your communication partner's needs and wants: Use both verbal and non-verbal clues to develop a sense of what your partner wants, considers important, and does not want. With practice, you will surprise yourself at the number of clues that jump out at you.

Acknowledge the needs and wants of others: It is important to let others know by your words or your actions that you acknowledge their wants and needs. This lets them know that you are prepared to find a mutually agreeable solution. It encourages them to acknowledge your goals as well.

Become a partner in the search for the solution: You have your goals; your partner has his or her goals. Your task is to cooperate in finding a solution. This allows both of you to stand behind the results, because you both have contributed meaningfully to the solution.

Acknowledge the results: If you have followed the above steps, this was a solution where everybody 'won.' Cement the agreement with a sincere acknowledgement of your accomplishment. Give the credit to your partner, but pat yourself on the back, too.

An Example

When my husband and I married, he was visiting this country and had no right to stay and work. We planned to visit the United Kingdom for our honeymoon, so we visited the local Immigration office to get the papers we would need to return. After our honeymoon, we went through customs in St. Louis, where we were told that, despite our paperwork, Paul could not re-enter the United States. By leaving, he had forfeited his chance to apply for a green card from inside the United States. He would have to return to England and apply from there.

This was not what we had been told in San Diego. This was not only personally distressing for both of us; it was also urgent. Just the thought of Paul's being deported on the spot made us more than a little desperate. Paul and I called up everything we knew about communication to find a solution that suited everyone.

Our overall goal was to get home to San Diego together. Standing in our way was a very well-informed officer of the federal government. It was apparent from his actions and his demeanor that he was not acting maliciously. Nevertheless, he did take his job and his responsibilities very seriously. He kept an emotional distance and attempted to remain impartial. We needed his cooperation if we were to get home. Our intention, therefore, was to involve him in the solution.

We started by making sure that the officer knew that we respected him and his authority. We make a point of calling him "Sir" and acknowledging that he had to do his job professionally. We allowed him to keep his impartiality while we asked him to help us find a solution. "Obviously you know the codes in detail. What interpretation of the codes would allow Paul to re-enter the country?" As he began to see that he could achieve his aims and help us achieve ours, the officer began to work with us.

We paid close attention to the pace of the officer's conversation. He began to quote favorable codes by serial number and equally quickly to quote conflicting codes which would negate the first code. We simply listened, allowing our hopes to join with his as we considered each new suggestion and our disappointment to mirror his as each proved to be inappropriate. We wanted to let the officer know by our responses that we were paying attention to his words and encouraging him to continue.

Before long, the officer had become our partner in search of a solution. We acknowledged that he had to do his job and he acknowledged that we were sincere and honest in our desire to return home. We found that we could share the same agenda. It didn't take long for the officer to find a solution once we were on the same table. We acknowledged his need to confer with his superiors before he passed us through. He, in turn, seemed genuinely convinced that meeting our needs was the best way to do his job. We parted satisfied that we all had done the right thing.

Tools for Understanding

It is often a good idea to make sure that you and your partner share the same understanding about your agreement. Especially when additional action must be taken, your agreement must be on-going. Don't assume that your agreement means the same thing to each of you just because you seem to understand each other.

Remember, any two people are likely to have completely different maps of reality. Because each of you interprets life based on your own previous experiences, you may also interpret your agreement differently. We can never guarantee that we completely understand each other, but there are some safeguards we can take to get as close to an understanding as possible.

Restate your agreement at the end of your communication: "I think we are in agreement, but just to be sure let's go over it. I will get the contract prepared for you to review by the thirteenth. You will look at it, make any corrections and get it back to me with your signature by the fifteenth. Then we will meet again on the seventeenth, when our goal will be to develop an approach for the project. It that correct?"

Put your agreement and your expectations in writing: "Here are the additions and corrections we discussed and agreed to in our meeting last Thursday. I look forward to receiving a completed copy of the program by next Wednesday's meeting."

Restate your agreement at the beginning of your next communication: "When we ended our phone call last week, we agreed that we both needed more time to develop the best solution to the design problem. How do you feel about it today?"

At times, no matter what you do, what you say, or how effectively you confirm your agreement, communication still breaks down. These times require additional communication. You will need to retrace your steps to find the source of confusion. The more effective you were at creating the original written or verbal agreement with your partner, the easier it will be to retrace your steps.

We all have a certain amount of resistance to taking extra steps to assure clear communication, but the more important the communication, the more important it is to take these extra steps. If your success at work depends upon clear communication, get used to employing the agreement checks suggested above. Even if you don't mind missed appointments or blank stares when you bring up a subject you have already talked about, clear understanding is still important. It is never too early or too late to begin using effective communication.

Let Your Fingers Do the Talking

What we *don't* say in words is just as important as what we do. Non-verbal communication covers everything we say without using words. We all learn about non-verbal communication even before we know that there is such a thing as communication. A child feels threatened when another child stares at his ice cream cone. A teenager feels uncomfortable when she feels the ogle of a classmate from across the room. An employee says "Yes, I'll do it," but his clenched teeth and icy stare say, *You're a jerk, boss.*

Should we trust our ears or our feelings? Both. But to understand non-verbal communication, we need to learn how to trust our feelings.

How often have you realized, when a situation turned bad, that you hadn't listened to the little voice inside that had been trying to get your attention? Your feelings sensed something amiss. Sometimes it is impossible to put your finger on the source of concern. Sometimes we dismiss the concern as unimportant because we can't attach a rational explanation to the feeling. Sometimes the feeling disappears after a time only to resurface later. Nonverbal communication is almost impossible to control, which is why it is usually the most honest.

Few if any of us can successfully hide our non-verbal communication. One well-known and respected television news program recently interviewed a specialist in non-verbal communication. While this expert responded verbally with a resounding "yes, absolutely," her head moved from side to side in a classic non-verbal "no" response. Our physical selves can reveal more information than we might want. This is another reason why being clear about your own intentions is so important. Without a clear acknowledgment of your intentions, you may find your body sending one message and your words sending a completely different one.

When you see what appears to be a conflict between another's verbal and non-verbal communication, be sure to acknowledge it, at least to yourself. You may be able to confirm the conflicted information by rephrasing a statement or question. If it is appropriate, ask the person directly to explain the apparent conflict. It may be caused by something as minor as a wandering mind or fatigue. But it also may indicate a personal conflict surrounding the issue at hand. If so, you will need to find a new way to handle the communication or resolve the conflict which the other feels.

Nonverbal communication is not the same thing as 'body language.' Interpreting body language can get pretty complicated, as the many books on subjects like Neurolinguistic Programming illustrate. But understanding non-verbal communication is both much less complicated and much more sophisticated. At its simplest, it is merely becoming sensitive to what you feel when you hear or speak to another person. The only requirements are that you listen effectively (see Chapter 3) and that you trust yourself to be alert to discrepancies.

Making sure you are understood requires that you understand the outlines of your communication partner's map of reality. It requires that you make a commitment to communicating clearly with both verbal and sometimes written confirmation. It requires a clear intention to make your verbal and non-verbal communications speak the same message honestly. It requires that you listen openly so that you can hear what is being said and feel what you are feeling. And finally it requires you to act on the knowledge you gain.

Fortunately, as we'll see in later chapters, all it takes is practice.

5

Recreating vs. Repeating Information

Theater-goers often have two questions for actors: *How did you memorize all those lines?* and *Doesn't it get boring repeating the same lines night after night?*

If the lines had nothing to do with each other, it would be impossible for anyone without a photographic memory to do the memorizing. But most actors will tell you that the secret lies in the fact that the the words actually have a great deal to do with each other. They are connected, held together by a mesh of the character's feelings, beliefs, opinions, and temperment...by the character's map of reality. And, the lines are connected to each other. They appear in the context of the other lines and events of the play, and they are generally repeated in response to the words or action of another character. While memorizing is sometimes necessary, it is not as difficult as it might seem to those who only watch the actors perform.

Repeating the same lines night after night is also not as difficult as it might seem. Actor have a battery of 'tricks' to keep the performance interesting. The common secret among all the tricks, actors will tell you, is to recreate, not just to repeat, the events of the play each time they perform. This means acting as if the performer were actually the character being portrayed.

Constantin Stanislavski, a Russian actor, director, and teacher, developed the *As If* principal during the early part of this century. His system is still taught today. Stanislavski recognized that if an actor understood how a character lived each moment, how the character breathed, thought, observed, spoke, moved, ate, and conversed—in short, if the actor lived on stage as if he or she were the character—then the actor would live each moment of the play as if he or she were experiencing it in person for the first time. Each night is a new discovery, and each audience sees a recreation, a new performance, a performance that looks as if it were being performed for the very first time.

Presenting As If

Stanislavski's *As If* principle also applies to presentation in everyday life. Learning to recreate information can bring new life to the words we say and the concepts we speak about. Suppose you are speaking with a new client who has never heard any of your information before. By speaking as if this were the first time you have ever presented this information with anyone, you can share your enthusiasm for your product with your client and invite your client to share your enthusiasm.

Presenting *As If* highlights the difference between repeating and recreating. To repeat is *to say again*, whereas to recreate is *to create anew*. To create anew, you have to go back to your original inspiration to guide your words and actions. What inspired you to go into the work you do, to write an article, or to call someone with an idea? Once we become involved in something, we often forget what inspired us in the first place. When we revisit that inspiration, we can revive the excitement once again. With this new-found reinspiration, we can share our enthusiasm with our audience much more easily.

For instance, helping someone understand a concept or idea by resurrecting the emotions of your first experience with the information will bring the two of you closer together. If you are speaking before a group, reliving your initial inspiration will help you establish a rapport with your audience. When you present your information as if you were hearing it for the first time, you will use words that are appropriate for your audience, who *are* hearing it for the first time. You will become much more sensitive to the audiences' ability to understand what you are saying than to your ability simply to put the information across.

Actors have to seek out the original inspiration to create belivable performances. They look beyond the written words in a script to find the impulse or inspiration for their character's dialogue. They search for the reason that their characters say what they say. Once actors understand why their character says something, they can decide how they should deliver the line in order to reflect their characters' original inspiration.

When you deliver a presentation, you are the character. The inspiration for the dialogue is yours, so you need to be familiar with your own inspiration. You also need to consider the realities of your audience, so you can deliver your message in a way that shares your inspiration and moves your listeners the way you were first moved.

For example, if I were making a presentation, I would first identify what is interesting, exciting, or anxiety-provoking about the information I want to share with the particular audience. This would help me understand the concerns of everyone in the audience. I would recall whatever gave me similar feelings so that I could set my immediate concerns aside and merge with my audience. I would acknowledge their fears in the body of my presentation. In fact, I would encourage reactions precisely because I am involved with the audience. I would use the skills and techniques presented in this book to speak directly to their eyes, ears, and emotions. Their expressions and their physical reactions would give me the feedback I needed to measure my success at involving them in my presentation. These reactions would tell me how successful I had been. As one of my clients once said, "You can smell it."

Speaking *as if for the first time* requires that you prepare your presentation sufficiently for you to be able to trust your knowledge of your subject and yourself. With your preparation in place, you can turn your attention completely to your audience, allowing yourself to live in their world for the duration of the encounter. The 'trick' is to prepare completely and then to involve yourself completely in the moment.

Comedy actors know that an audience is likely to laugh after they deliver certain lines. They are prepared to pause if laughter comes, but they know that if they pause in anticipation of a laugh they will kill the laughter. Why? Because an actor who presents a line knowing it to be funny is repeating, not recreating, stifling spontaneity and actually destroying the humor of the moment. On the other hand, when the actor speaks the line as if he had no thought for the reaction to it, the line will have the spontaneity, inspiration, and timing to make it funny. The audience will respond without being prompted.

When you are presenting effectively, presenting *as if for the first time*, you are going to get reactions from your audience. The reactions may be positive or negative, depending on your message. But one thing is predictable: the audience will have been involved and will understand your message.

As If *In Practice*

Andrea was an actress portraying a middle-aged woman who was having an affair with an eighteen-year-old man. Andrea had to understand the balancing act her character needed to perform with her emotions, her self-image, her personal growth, and her anger at her husband (an uncaring oaf). Andrea had never experienced the life of her character, but she knew the challenge of balancing conflicting needs and emotions. To prepare for her recreation each night, she concentrated on the way she was balancing different aspects of her own life. She also began, quite absentmindedly one day, to balance a salt shaker on some grains of salt while she was preparing mentally.

Andrea found the inspiration for her character very quickly with the help of this routine. She discovered that the salt shaker routine acted as a physical prompt which allowed her to go much further toward acting as if she were the character. This physical and mental activity became her nightly routine each and every night of the performance.

Daniel, an experienced attorney, knew his opening statements in the courtroom were not as inspiring as he wanted them to be. He routinely spoke down to the jurors. Yet he was reluctant to change his style, defending himself by saying that he needed to present himself as an attorney and an authority on the subject. He was afraid that the jury would see him as just another person.

Gradually, Daniel learned that if he used the language of his audience and spoke as if he were involved in what he was describing, he would be able to involve the jury in his story. He rehearsed and found that simple visualizations invariably synchronized his presentation and his message. In one case, he simply visualized the road where his client's accident took place as if he, Daniel, were driving the car. The crucial element was imagining that his children were in the back seat. With this visualization in mind, Daniel related completely to the horror his client felt, and he was able to communicate a clear, vivid picture to the jury.

To present *As If*, you need to concentrate moment by moment on your audience, whether that audience is a single person or a full room. To concentrate, you must trust yourself enough to abandon your self-consciousness and give your full attention to your audience. Your *As If* skills

build on the trust you develop as you come to understand yourself, your strengths and weaknesses, and your
communication goals. Presenting *As If* enables you to
speak a language that your audience will understand and
to use images and concepts that are meaningful to your
audience.

If you are satisfied with yourself, your ability to concentrate, and your willingness to establish rapport with
your audience, you are now ready to turn your mental
and emotional tools into physical and vocal expressiveness. The next two chapters will help you make sure that
you and your audience understand each other.

6

How To Say What You Mean

The voice is an overlooked asset. Like a fingerprint, it projects who we are, our unique feelings, our ideas, our hopes, and our dreams. It sends vocal pictures to others. Your voice can be a powerful tool. When you communicate well, your listeners translate your voice and words into images and incorporate them into their own maps of reality. Then they act on what you have said.

Ah, such a lovely picture of communication! If all communication were so dynamic we probably wouldn't have very many misunderstandings. Unfortunately, our speaking rarely takes on that kind of power. More often our meaning is forced through the cracks left by our listeners' lack of concentration, distractions, judgments, and boredom. Before we blame the listeners for this situation, though, consider the quality of the voice they are listening to. Is it fair to ask them to shut off their minds and simply listen, especially if we are speaking with an unexpressive or uninteresting voice? Why should they, when nothing in the quality of the voice beckons their attention?

Let Your Voice Stroke the Ear of the Listener.

My father used to stop everything to listen when one particular commentator spoke on the radio. "Paul Harvey could say 'shaving cream' and make it sound interesting." As a salesman, Dad intuitively understood the power of vocal gesture, something that Paul Harvey mastered as fully as anyone.

I learned what my father meant when I was twelve and attending children's theatre classes. My teacher, a retired opera singer who was attuned to the voice, recorded our voices so that we could understand vocal expression. I was devastated when I first heard my voice. It was high pitched and nasal, and it came out with this irritating Midwestern twang. My teacher didn't need to criticize my voice. I knew that I should never speak again. I walked home in a cloud of devastation and ate dinner as the mute I vowed to remain.

My self-imposed silence lasted only a day or so, but the impression changed me forever. I began listening to voices and deciding which ones were interesting or pleasing, and why. Only after I began studying theater as an undergraduate, however, did I learn that the voice can be a malleable tool, not simply a burden. In a class on the technical use of the voice, I learned that the voice can be shaped just as fully as the appearance. A whole new world of expression beckoned. I was relieved.

Anatomy of the Voice

What is the voice? Is it the sounds we make? Is it the way we use words to express our ideas? Actually, it is both. When we talk about the voice, we are talking about two things: the quality of the sound we create and the way we use sound to express meaning. Just as high quality fabric can be cheapened by poor workmanship, a pleasing voice can be wasted when it is used in an uninteresting way. By contrast, an ordinary voice in the mouth of a skillful speaker can contribute to a fascinating vocal presence.

The quality of a voice is influenced by a number of factors—heredity, bone structure, tension, and general attitude. Neither heredity nor bone structure can be changed. Attitude and stress, however, two other factors that can profoundly affect the voice, *can* be rechanneled. This chapter will introduce a number of techniques that can assist in this process.

Vocal Gesture

Physical gestures are movements used to express or emphasize ideas or emotions. Gesture is usually understood as something we do with our bodies or parts of our bodies, particularly our hands and arms. But gesture isn't limited to the body. It also applies to the voice. Just as we use our hands, fingers, arms, and heads to point or show our emotions, we use vocal gesture to point toward our intended meaning.

There are four basic tools of vocal gesture—the pitch of our voice, the pace of our speech, the variation of our volume, and the strategic use of pauses. Pitch is the frequency, or tone, of the voice. Pace is the rate and rhythm at which we speak. Volume is the loudness with which we say our words. And verbal pauses are the punctuation marks that spice up the whole conversation. Each of these, both alone and in combination, affects the way our words sound and the way our meaning is communicated.

In normal conversation, we use these tools naturally to make our verbal gestures. Unfortunately, when we need the skills most, our natural ability to gesture often eludes us. Tension is the villain, for both emotional and physical reasons. Muscles need to be relaxed in order to function at their best. The stress of tension tightens the muscles, especially at those times when relaxed muscles are what we need.

Fortunately, we can train the voice, through exercise, to deliver clear verbal gestures. These voice exercises are just as important for speakers as physical exercises are for athletes. Even if you already have a pleasant speaking voice, vocal exercises can both warm up your vocal chords, improve your verbal stamina, release the tension that can interfere with your performance, and make your presentations more effective and dramatic.

Vocal Mime

One effective way of training the voice is to do what a mime does to train the body. A mime is an artist who expresses ideas with the body alone. By definition, the mime does not use words.

Because the face is the most expressive part of the body, the mime trains with a mask on. This mask obscures the face and forces the mime to learn how to express with parts of the body other than the face. Learning how to coax expression out of the body can be frustrating at first. With practice, however, the mime learns some very powerful communication techniques.

Most of us depend upon our words to communicate our meaning and our faces to tell people how we feel. But, just as the mime covers the face to aid the expression of the physical self, we can put a mask on our words to keep our meaning from running the show.

A mask on words? The meaning we perceive from words comes not only from the individual word but from the words in combination. If we place a series of disconnected words together, creating a nonsensical series of sentences, our meaning becomes masked. It becomes possible to exercise the voice outside of meaning, just as the mime exercises the body without the face.

Exercise: The Vocal Mask

The paragraph below is composed of words strung together in a nonsensical fashion. But it is not without 'meaning.' This exercise will help you give 'meaning' to the random string of words. (I recommend that you tape yourself while you complete the exercise so you can hear the results and judge them for yourself.)

Read the paragraph out loud. Change pitch on each syllable by raising or lowering the tone of your voice.

Read the words again, this time changing pace on each syllable by speeding up and slowing down the flow of the sounds.

Now, read the words, changing volume on each syllable and varying the loudness of your reading.

Finally, read the paragraph a fourth time. Combine changes in pitch, pace, and volume to find 'meaning' in this silly grouping of words. Throw in an occasional pause, especially where you sense that a pause would lend an important emphasis. The 'meaning' will come if you simply change your pitch, pace, and volume.

Tired trusting teased trees. See pest past quell misery. Westward boundary waiting privately traveling airborne wounded trust. Exceptionally gain avant-garde random access inward how vehement incipient waste causes patent pain. Lustful castigations crest over comrades careful twilight. Ingenious laboratory awaken answers vehement passport. Therefore, past present forevermore equivalent timeless passion.

Lungs, Chest, And Ribs

The voice comes from several physical areas, each of which can be exercised to improve overall vocal prowess. The diaphragm, ribs, and lungs, then the chest, shoulders, and throat, and finally the jaw, lips, teeth, tongue, and facial bone structure—all contribute to the sounds we create. The way we stand or sit also makes a difference. A brief look at each component will help make clear the way each contributes to the whole.

Vocal power is the ability of the voice to reflect a speaker's intent. While breathing is crucial for effective vocal power, most people breathe as if they were breath misers. This shallow breathing actually saps vocal power. Think about the last time you had something really important to say. What was your breathing like? Many of us stop breathing almost entirely, holding our breath and taking in only enough air to keep us from passing out. We don't resume breathing until we take that nice, deep, relaxing breath at the end of our moment in the spotlight.

The time for deep breathing is *before* you speak. This centers your energy and balances your mind. The breathing exercise below will help you learn the correct way to breath, a way which calms your physical self as it calms your mind and emotions.

Exercise: Effective Breathing

Sit in a chair which has arms and a back. Let the back of the chair support your back and the arms of the chair support your arms. Place your right hand on your abdomen and your left hand on your upper chest.

Push all the air in your lungs out through your mouth. Quickly inhale through your nose, feeling your abdomen expand with your right hand while your chest (left hand) remains still. Hold this breath as long as you can, releasing it when you must through your mouth. Remain empty of air for as long as you can before you have to inhale.

Now breath normally and notice how your diaphragm under your right hand expands naturally. Repeat this exercise three times, taking time to breath naturally between each repetition.

The lungs are the bellows that produce the voice. They work like sacks or balloons. As the diaphragm expands, it creates a vacuum which forces the lungs to expand and suck in air. The less the lungs expand, the less air is available to the voice. One of the limits on the ability of the lungs to expand is the ribs, the cage in which the lungs rest. To make more room for the lungs, we need to learn how to expand our ribs when we breathe.

Exercise: Unlocking the Ribs

Repeat the "Effective Breathing" exercise above. This time, notice your rib cage and pay attention to its movement or lack of movement. Expand your back along the chair so you can feel the pressure of your ribs as you breathe. (Alternatively, you can stand, placing one hand on your abdomen and the other on your side).

As you breath, feel for pressure against the hand along your side. If you feel no pressure, you probably are not expanding your ribs. Using only your muscles, push your ribs out to the side. You may not be able to move your rib cage very much at first, but continue pushing your ribs apart until you can feel them expand.

Now breathe naturally and feel air rush into your lungs as your ribs expand. Relax your abdomen, expand your diaphragm, and allow air to move deeply into your lungs. Expanding your ribs, chest, and abdomen, releases unnecessary tension and creates as much space as possible for your lungs and diaphragm.

Shoulders, Upper Chest, and Arms

When you breath in a relaxed and open way, it is much easier to relax your upper chest, shoulders, and arms. Tension in these areas also prevents the lungs from expanding freely. By releasing your shoulders, arms, and chest, you allow sound to touch the muscles, bones, and cartilage and create vibrations known as resonance.

To experience resonance, place one hand on your chest about six inches above your solar plexus. Speak out loud and, with your hand, feel the vibrations you produce. If you don't feel any vibrations or feel them only sporadically, make a low *ahhhhhh* sound. The lower the pitch, the more you will feel the vibration, because lower pitches, which vibrate at a lower frequency with a wider wave length, are easier to feel. If you do feel the vibration, raise your pitch as high as you can until you can no longer feel the vibrations.

When you present, create as much resonance as possible, regardless of the pitch of your voice. Why? Because resonance is a physical phenomenon that can be felt. It expands the sound of your voice and fills the room with a perceptible presence. Resonance strokes the ear of the listener and reminds the audience that you are speaking. The more resonance you can create, the more you can keep the attention of your audience.

Exercise: Releasing the Shoulders

Sit comfortably in a chair with your hands in your lap and your palms down. Slowly slide your hand toward your knees, stopping every few inches to release and drop your shoulders. When your hands reach your knees (or as close to your knees as you can get them), release and drop your shoulders one more time.

Now slowly raise your outstretched hands vertically, stopping periodically to release and drop your shoulders. When your arms and hands are finally stretched directly over your head, release and drop your shoulders once again and breathe in and out several times, releasing and dropping your shoulders with each breath. Finally, drop your arms and hands to your knees once again and slowly pull your hands back to your lap.

The Jaw

Don't be surprised if you also notice tension in your throat, neck, or jaw. Most of us hold some degree of tension in these areas all the time, and this tension can also interfere with our ability to express with vocal gestures.

Pay particular attention to your jaw. The jaw must be open and flexible to help shape sound as it moves into your mouth. Tightness in the jaw can undo all the centering and relaxing you have accomplished so far.

Exercise: Release the Jaw

Hold your chin with one hand and use your hand only to move your jaw up and down. If you feel any resistance, place one or two fingers on your jaw muscle (where the upper and lower jaws are hinged together) and massage the muscle for about thirty seconds. Again, move your jaw with your hand alone, then move your lower jaw forward and back for about thirty seconds. Now repeat the exercise and notice the difference.

The jaw is one of several sound 'shapers,' or articulaters, that work together to help turn sound into meaning. Others are your lips, teeth, and tongue. These, too, except for your teeth, will also benefit from exercise. The more vibrant and flexible these articulaters are, the better able you will be to shape your sounds into dynamic words and gestures.

Exercise: Articulation

The purpose of this exercise is to help you enunciate and articulate your words more smoothly and clearly. To do this, you need to relax the muscles of your jaw, your lips, and your tongue while you repeat the tongue-twisting sequence of letters below.

Create short, sharp sounds while you voice the following letters at very low volume. Repeat the letters, increasing the pace but not the volume, until you can go no faster.

P, P, B, B, T, T, D, D, K, K, G, G.
P, P, B, B, T, T, D, D, K, K, G, G.
P, P, B, B, T, T, D, D, K, K, G, G.

Now, repeat the following nonsensical paragraph in a whisper. Be careful to articulate the consonants sharply and clearly. Repeat the paragraph with increasing speed but not volume until you can go no faster.

Tee, Toe, TiP oF The Tongue, eL, eL, eL, eL, eL, Ssssssss, Pah.
Tee, Toe, TiP oF The Tongue, eL, eL, eL, eL, eL, Ssssssss, Pah.
Tee, Toe, TiP oF The Tongue, eL, eL, eL, eL, eL, Ssssssss, Pah.

Very slowly and in a low volume repeat the paragraph that follows. As above, increase your speed but not your volume until you can go no faster.

Red Leather, Yellow Leather, Red Leather, Yellow Leather.
Red Leather, Yellow Leather, Red Leather, Yellow Leather.
Red Leather, Yellow Leather, Red Leather, Yellow Leather.

Your Face and Its Muscles and Bones
The final set of influences on our sounds are the nose, cheeks, forehead, and the rest of the face. The face has hundreds of tiny muscles, each of which is capable of holding tension. Releasing facial tension improves your ease of articulation and your ability to project a resonating sound.

Exercise: Pressure Points on Your Face

If you are wearing glasses or contact lenses, remove them. Place your forefingers on the bone of your lower eye sockets at the point closest to your nose. Press for two seconds then release. Press again and release; press a third time and release. Move your fingers a small distance toward the outer part of your eye and repeat the press/release process. Continue moving your fingers along the lower bone of your eye socket, stopping every quarter inch or so to repeat the press-release cycle. When you have reached the outer edge of the eye, place your thumbs at the innermost point of the upper eye socket. Repeat pressing and releasing on the upper eye socket, using your thumbs instead of your forefingers.

Now place your forefingers at the innermost points of your cheekbones. Press in and up with your fingers for two seconds and release. Repeat two times. Move your fingers toward the outer sides of your face, stopping every half inch or so to press, hold for two seconds, and release, repeating three times at each point along the cheekbone.

When you reach the outermost area of your cheekbones, place your forefingers just below the bone to the jaw muscle. Massage the muscle for thirty seconds. Tuck your thumbs under your jaw just below your ears on either side of your face and rub the bone. Slowly move your fingers toward your chin, stopping every inch or so to rub the bone.

Place your forefingers together at the bridge of your nose. While exerting constant pressure along each finger and toward your skin, push your fingers straight up your forehead and toward your hairline. When you reach your scalp, flatten all your fingers on your entire forehead and, continuing to exert pressure, pull your hands slowly toward the outer sides of your face. Repeat twice more.

With a relaxed face, it is possible to create sound and resonance from the facial 'mask.' This is the area formed roughly by the forehead, cheeks, nose, and mouth. Relaxing the face allows the mask to resonate as we speak, working with the resonation of the chest to fill the room with vibrating tones. It also helps you to project your message with a clear and confident sound so that everyone in the room can hear and trust what you are saying.

The Vocal Gesture Package

There is more to a presentation than an open, relaxed, resonating sound. How we say our words can be just as important. We gesture with our words and sounds, just as we gesture with our arms and facial expressions. Our pitch, our pace, our volume, our pauses, all affect how our message is received.

Vocal gestures come naturally when we consciously recognize our intention. As we have seen, we have to be clear about what we are trying to say and what we want our audience to learn. Once we know our intention, we can begin to paint verbal pictures of that intention.

Even the specific words we choose can affect the way our message is perceived. Words have both sound and meaning, and both qualities can become tools for expressing our feelings and achieving our intentions. Shakespeare was a master at this. In all of his plays, you will find only one single stage direction. Yet actors and audiences have understood his plays for hundreds of years. In large measure, the reason is that Shakespeare chose his words, not just for their meaning, but also for their sound and their affective power.

The more you use words as gestures, the better able you will be to select words that communicate your feelings. Consider the following extreme examples. Notice how the second of each pair communicates the same message as the first, but so much more.

A. *We walked down the block at dusk.*
B. *We strolled casually past the freshly mown lawns, breathing in the moist, late-afternoon smells.*

A. *The adversity took its toll on her.*
B. *She trudged through the conflict, sinking deeper into a mire of anger and despair with each step she took.*

What picture do the first statements paint? The second statements? Do the words beckon to be spoken differently? Does either statement add more texture and meaning? Is intent more clearly defined in either statement?

Without vocal gesture, communication would be terribly dull and uninspiring. What gives pizzazz to communication is the vocal gesture that gives texture and depth to intention.

Exercise: Vocal Gesture

Practice the following vocal gesture exercise until you feel comfortable changing the pitch, pace, volume, and pause of vocal gesture. As you practice, you will find it becomes increasingly easier to clarify your intention before speaking. You will also find your mind focussing more and more clearly on the present moment. (Again, I recommend that you record yourself doing this exercise so you can hear the results.)

Repeat the following statement:

She walked up the stairs.

Make clear the direction she walked by raising your pitch on the word up. Can you find another vocal gesture to emphasize her direction?

Change your intention. Make it clear that she didn't run up the stairs. For example, try pausing slightly before the word walked, raising your pitch on the word and adding a bit of volume.

Now emphasize that she walked quickly. "She" (pause slightly, then increase your pace gradually with each of the following words while increasing your pitch) "walked up the stairs".

Don't be frustrated if you find vocal gesture challenging. Old habits that get in the way can take effort to unlearn. Be gentle and understanding with yourself during the process. Enjoy the process. It is part of getting to know yourself *As If.*

7

Looking The Part

In ancient Greece, plays were staged in huge amphitheaters before thousands of spectators. Actors had to project their voices and meanings so that even the inebriated theater-goer in the last row could follow the play. To do this, actors often wore oversized masks with megaphone-like mouths which amplified their voices and made their characters' identities apparent. They also developed techniques of exaggerating their physical expressions to send the appropriate emotional messages to the audience.

Today we have microphones to amplify our voices and television cameras to capture close-up images. But that doesn't mean we no longer need to project physically in accordance with our intentions. We still have to speak the same message with our voice and our body. We still must learn to project our messages so that they hit our audience where we are aiming.

Gesture Toward Your Intention

Every presentation has a physical dimension. It is there whether you are conscious of it or not, and it is part of your message even if you don't know what your body is saying. Powerful presentation involves a conscious integration of words and gestures so that both project the same meaning. If you have followed the suggestions throughout the previous chapters, you have already begun integrating your words and your gestures. This chapter will help you consolidate what you have learned.

Follow the Leader

If you are focused on your intentions, your body can follow suit. When you are emotionally and mentally in tune with your intention, your words and actions are likely to be in harmony. And when your words and action are in harmony, you and your message will have integrity.

Your body can help communicate your intent, especially if you take the time to rehearse your message. By repeating an action until your body remembers the new process instead of the old one, you can teach your body to send physical messages that agree with your verbal message. Don't expect the process to work overnight (although it could). It might take a little practice to incorporate the new message, but keep with it. The results are well worth the effort.

The Expressive Triangle

Expression comes from the entire body and particularly from the area known as the *expressive triangle*, which is formed by the head, shoulders, arms, and upper chest. We all use this expressive triangle to reflect, amplify, and punctuate the messages we send with our words and vocal gestures. With your eyes and face, for example, you look directly at individual members of the audience while your face expresses multiple levels of emotion and intellectual understanding. You lean your head forward or backward or turn it from side to side. You show your audience that you are listening by turning your head and literally "lending an ear."

One of the most common blocks to physical expressiveness—tension—frequently lurks in the shoulders. Most people hold tension in the shoulders and the back of the neck. Holding tension is not in itself a negative thing. Holding it beyond a certain point, however, can be harmful to our health and detrimental to our expression. Free and loose, the shoulders make the rest of the triangle express more effectively. Constricted and blocked, the shoulders become a wall that separates speaker from audience. Chapters 6 and 8 discuss several things you can do to reduce any tension you might be holding in this part of your expressive triangle.

Gestures with the arms lend a certain drama and appeal to a presentation. Imagine trying to listen to a speaker who stands board-stiff while talking. As a general rule, the size of your gestures should be proportional to the size of the audience. The reason for this is fairly obvious. The larger the audience, the farther away some individuals may be sitting, and the farther away an audience member is, the larger your gesture needs to be simply to stay in proportion to the distances involved. At the same time, however, the greater the distance, the simpler the gesture needs to be. A rather complex gesture which makes perfect sense in a one-on-one conversation will be much too elaborate when viewed from the back of the auditorium.

Even trained actors need to be reminded of this. When the late Joseph Papp first cast television actors on the stage, audiences were often disappointed. Many of the actors had been trained to act only before the camera. When performing on stage, they had to learn the hard way that the gestures that had made them so successful before the camera—a simple twitch of an eye or a tiny tilt of the head, for example—could not be seen past the first row in the theater.

The last component of the expressive triangle is the chest. This is the foundation to which the other components are attached. How you hold your chest can make or break your efforts to achieve the look of a good presentation. When your chest is collapsed, for example, or when it is held too high or protruded too far, it is difficult for the rest of your expressive triangle to do its job.

In general, whether you are presenting to a single individual or a large group, the most effective way to hold your chest is to imagine that a spotlight is embedded in your chest from your neck to your sternum. As you face your audience, 'shine' this spotlight out so that you bathe your audience in light. When you are addressing a single person, shine the light directly on that person. When you are speaking to a group, shift the light from area to area.

The Rest of the Body

During a successful presentation, your entire body should follow the lead of your expressive triangle. Your ribs, for example, which are so important for the production of your voice, must be open and expansive if your spotlight is to shine brightly. Likewise, if your chest is caved in, your ribs will not be able to expand in order to project your voice effectively. (This is yet another reason to do the vocal warm-up exercises discussed in the last chapter.)

Even how you stand and how you move your legs and feet can affect your ability to communicate your message. Constantin Stanislavski, the grandfather of contemporary acting technique, discovered that the truly inspired—and inspiring—actors planted their feet firmly on the ground as if they literally trusted the ground to support them. Similarly, Matthius Alexander discovered that expression is facilitated if the weight is rooted. Giving full weight directly to the ground releases the upper body to express more fully.

Imagine that a set of large electrical plugs is attached to the bottom of your feet. Keeps these plugs inserted all the way into the ground at all times. When you walk, plug in with each step. When you reach your destination, plug in again. Before you make a presentation remind yourself that you are giving your full weight to the earth and that the earth will support you as long as you are plugged all the way in.

The Sum of the Parts

Like the voice, which has pace, pitch, volume, and pause, a body gesture is a collection of parts that, together, make up the whole package. These parts are: the size of movement, the pace of movement, the repetition of movement, and the lack of movement. In addition, movement serves at least one other purpose: it takes the place of words. Physical gestures add emphasis and meaning to your verbal message and lend a visual component to your presentation. Use physical gesture and vary the components in the same way as you would use verbal gestures. It gives visual punctuation to your communication.

We have already seen how the size of the movement can affect a presentation. The size of movements and gestures must increase as the size of the audience increases. But there are other reasons to diversify the size of gestures and movements. Variety in size, for example, can create enthusiasm, it can focus an audience's attention narrowly, or it can add emphasis where you need to.

The pace of your movement, like the pace of your voice, moves your listeners toward your intended goal. Make the pace of your movement commensurate with the pace of your voice. Speed up your gestures as your voice speeds up; slow your gestures down as the intensity of your words goes down. Varying the pace of your movement, like varying the pace of your words, helps your audience to continue paying attention to your presentation.

Repeating the same word or phase can help cement meaning for the audience. Repetition in gesture can have the same effect. Linking an idea or a thought to a specific gesture, for example, gives your audience a visual cue to remember what you want them to remember. It can also act as an attention grabber in much the same way as a familiar melody in a piece of music can snap a listener's drifting attention back to the music.

The absence of a gesture can also have dramatic effect. For example, it can communicate to an audience that you are making a transition between ideas and that there is a new idea coming. At the same time, it can have the same impact that a pause in speech has, lending suspense to or anticipation about what you are going to present.

Movement can also substitute for words. When a gesture is coupled with an idea, the gesture can be performed on its own and the audience will 'hear' the word. Think of the common gestures we all understand—a shrug of the shoulders or a facial grimace, for example. These gestures do not need to be accompanied by words at all. Likewise, a gesture can allow the audience to think of the correct response all on its own. Gestures can symbolize very complex, interwoven ideas in a way that words simply cannot.

As practice, imagine you are a sales manager speaking to a room filled with salespeople. You are going to tell them:

Last years' profits soared above our competitor's.

How would you use gestures to convey your congratulations and instill enthusiasm?

One way might be to move your left hand quickly and positively to the left when you say "Last years' profits." Then, holding your left hand stationary, move your right hand and arm in a slow arc above your head while you say, "soared above our competitor's." Hold this position for a moment before you move on to your next thought.

Now, suppose last year's profits were very good, but this year things have been different. How might you use gesture to reinforce this message?

You might start by moving your left hand, thumb first, to the left when you say "Last year's profit." When you say, "soared above," move the left hand quickly upward about ten or twelve inches while you say, "soared above." Then dropping your hand and arm quickly to your side, stand still, look directly at several individual members of the audience, and say, "our competitor's." After a brief, silent pause, move your right hand up and away from your body, palm-up, as if you are saying, "What's up this year, guys?"

Finally, how would you communicate in gestures that you don't understand what changed between last year and this year but that you are open to explanations from your listeners?

While you say the entire statement, you could slowly shrug your shoulders while opening your palms to your audience.

The possibilities of incorporating gestures in your presentations are endless. Don't try to plan every movement and gesture before you speak. But do practice gestures until they become natural parts of your presentation. Practice until they become part of you, then trust yourself to make effective and appropriate use of gestures. Your audience will notice the difference.

8

Turn Fear Into Excitement

Stage fright is a perfectly natural reaction, even for people who make their livings standing before audiences. How many actors stand backstage before a production wondering why they put themselves through such agony? How many resolve that "This will be my last production?" And how many then forget their promise from the moment the curtain goes up until they began the ritual all over again the following night?

Good Energy, Bad Energy

For some, stage fright is an energizing experience. Many actors believe they would not be able to perform without nervous energy. They believe their nervousness drives their creativity. And, they may be right. These actors have developed the ability to turn fear and nervousness into excitement. They use the adrenalin that charges their bodies to provide extra energy and commitment to their performance.

Most normal people also create adrenalin, but the effect it has is often quite different. Many people turn nervousness into fear, creating doubts about their abilities. Unlike the actors whose fear and nervousness sends the message to their muscles to open, expand, and express, many people tell their muscles to shut down and become small and protected. This makes performance much more difficult. Fear and immobilization are normal and natural responses to anxiety. They are also unnecessary.

Residual Tension

Recall from Chapter Two that there is a close relationship between mental attitude and the nervous system. The words and images we use while speaking to ourselves can influence the way we perform. In a self-reinforcing manner, repetitive performance establishes patterns of performance. Other things being equal, our future performances will mirror our past performances. Whether our patterns serve us well or undermine us will depend, in part, on the mental attitudes we have learned to bring to our presentation. Our goal should be to preserve the positive connections, those patterns which contribute positively to our effectiveness, and to let go of the rest.

Consider the cat, an animal whose nervous system almost always produces appropriate reactions to physical or mental stress. The cat lounges peacefully, stretching out lazily on the front porch. Suddenly, a dog barks. The cat immediately leaps to all fours, shortens the muscles at the base of its neck, pulls it head back, tightens its stomach, and arches its back. The cat is ready to take on the challenge. Then it realizes that the dog is behind a fence. The cat releases the tension in its neck and stomach, stretches back out, and resumes its nap. It moves on to the next moment, letting go of any left-over tension from what has just happened.

We can learn to be like the cat, releasing the residual tensions that hamper our ability to pay attention to the task at hand. The challenge is that most of us are not even aware of the residual tension we carry around with us. But carry it we do, often to our own detriment. Tension, along with its associated paralysis, undermines our ability to be present in the moment.

This is no surprise to actors and others who depend on the cooperation of body and mind. Athletes, for example, know that excessive tension can tighten muscles, inhibit motion, and devastate performance. Sales people know that tension and negative thinking can guarantee the failure of a sales presentation. Students know that stress and doubts at test time can undo days of solid preparation.

With a little practice, you can learn to identify when you are holding residual tension. Pay attention while you go through your ordinary, everyday activities. Study your body's responses to physical and emotional situations. Be aware of the little things that are so easy to take for granted. How do you hold yourself? Are your shoulders hunched or curved? Do you feel any pressure in your legs or groin? How tightly do you hold your mouth shut?

Next time you are driving, for example, spend a little time observing. How tightly do you hold the steering wheel, for example? Do you grip the wheel with more effort than necessary? Try to relax your grip until you can find the gentlest grip needed to drive safely. Do you tighten your shoulders while you are driving? If so, see if you can release the tension and let your arms and hands do the work. Is your neck tight or your jaw jutting forward? Try to release some of this tension by rocking your head up and down or slowly rotating your head in a large circle (but only when the car is stopped!). How deep is your breathing? Make sure you inhale and exhale fully, without straining. See if you can learn to feel more relaxed on the road.

You can do the same thing while you are working at a desk. Pay attention to your arms, shoulders, neck, and jaw, and try to release the tension in the same way you did behind the steering wheel. If you are using a keyboard, notice how relaxing your arms and shoulders can actually help your fingers do the work. If you are writing by hand, notice what your body is doing while your hand is moving. Are you settling into the chair, or are you resisting it? Are your feet relaxed and in full contact with the floor, or are they pushing against it? Try to release all unnecessary muscle activity and tension and use only the muscles needed to perform the activity.

Releasing The Tension

Releasing habitual patterns of holding stress requires constant awareness. You may find that the tension you have just released from your shoulders, for example, soon comes back again. As you become more aware of the feedback your body sends you about tension, you will be better able to release the stress as soon as it appears.

Our bodies were meant to be fluid and flexible. When we learn to release tension continuously throughout the day, we can maintain our fluidity. Actors have learned how to release tension and free up their potential. Many of their techniques are readily available for anyone to use.

One 'stage secret' is to release the muscles you are about to use. This is called the *release/engage process*, and one of the best ways to do it is simply to walk. Go through the following walking exercise several times. After a while, you will begin using your muscles economically and minimizing the unnecessary buildup of tension. Plus, you will gain the benefits every time you walk.

Exercise: Walking

Stand up and relax all of the muscles that you do not need for holding yourself upright. Very slowly move one leg forward, paying attention to the muscles that are needed and those that are engaged but not necessary. Release the unnecessary muscles, working to use only those muscles that you really need for walking.

Practicing this in slow motion several times. Then begin moving naturally. As you walk, continue to release unnecessary tension by paying attention to the following guidelines:

• Make solid contact between your feet and the earth.

- Allow your knees to remain fluid and flexible.
- Allow your hips to remain released and flexible.
- Breathe fully and effortlessly in rhythm with your gait.
  - Swing your arms easily and naturally at your sides.
  - Keep your rib cage open and your "spotlight" (see Chapter 7) shining forward.
  - Allow your shoulders to take up as much space as possible.
    - Let your neck and head remain flexible and relaxed.
    - Finally, while you are walking, imagine that a string attached to the crown of your head lifts your upper body in a puppet-like motion as you walk.

In order to turn fear into excitement, you must release the memories of fears. These are often held in the body long after the stressful event has passed. When you hold on to these old experiences of fear, your body relives the old memory during your new experiences. Getting to know your body and feeling the effect of releasing unnecessary holding patterns helps you reverse this pattern and turn the fear into energy. If you let your adrenalin fuel your excitement instead of your dread, you will be able to respond to excitement with anticipation and openness and integrate your emotions with your message.

Thoughts And Presentation

Your mind is your strongest ally. Philosophers, psychologists, and gurus of all sorts have taught us that anything we can imagine we can achieve. But we have to imagine it first, make it real in our minds first, before the results can follow. If you feel fear when you speak, it is because fear is real in your mind. If you feel excitement, enthusiasm, and anticipation, then they become real, not your fears. External results will follow.

What follows is one step-by-step process for transforming fears into excitement. Read through this visualization often enough for you to be able to recreate it in your own mind. Read it into a tape recorder if playing it back will help you work through the exercise. Tailor it, if need be, to your own needs. Then practice it whenever you face a stressful presentation or other difficult situation.

Exercise: Turn Fear Into Excitement

Sit in a comfortable position, but do not lie down. (One of our minds' most effective ways of blocking change is to fall asleep.) Close your eyes and visualize your body as an empty shell. See the outline of your body, which is becoming transparent. As soon as you can see through your body, imagine that a tiny replica of yourself is inside. This Tiny You is going to cleanse your body of tension.

Tiny You is using a tiny brush to do a thorough cleaning of your insides. Starting at the skull, Tiny You moves down through your neck, shoulders, chest, back, stomach, intestines, hips, thighs, knees, calves, ankles and feet. At the bottom of your feet, Tiny You opens a door and sweeps out all the debris.

Now, Tiny You surveys your body. If any areas still need attention, Tiny You takes the tiny brush and vigorously brushes the spots that still hold tension. Notice as the tension falls from the walls of your body. What color is it? What shape is it? How do you feel as it is released? When your body has been completely cleaned of tension, it is thoroughly transparent. Tiny You plugs your feet into the ground.

A clear tube now descends from the heavens and fits over your head like a crown. It connects securely but not tightly and stays connected even when your head changes position. Once it is in place, Tiny You moves to your skull and gently pushes the top of your head open. Any fears or anxieties that still remain in your body magically float up through your open skull and into the tube. These emotions rise into the ethers and wait there safely until you want or need them back.

Your body is finally empty, and a pure white mist of inspiration moves down the tube to fill your body with a cleansing, healing power. Any tension or emotion that reappears is gently transformed into gray smoke and floats up the tube while pure white mist moves down to replace it. This fluid movement of white mist replacing gray smoke is continuous and constant until no trace of gray smoke remains.

Breath deeply and fully and enjoy the process. Notice how you feel. Notice when Tiny You discovers hidden tension. Notice what allows you to let it go.

Now imagine that the pure and open you is standing before your audience. Tiny You is there to continue the process as you speak. You know that Tiny You will be there to support you even when your attention is transferred to your audience.

Visualize this audience. See their eyes. See them looking at you with great interest. See them listening to your every word. See them caring about what you say.

Every now and then, shift your attention to Tiny You and congratulate Tiny You for doing such a good job of keeping you free of tension and filled with the pure white mist of inspiration. Thank Tiny You and assure it of your trust. Then pay attention to your audience again, knowing that if you should fall prey to anxiety, Tiny You will be there to help you overcome the moment and move on to the next.

Continue this visualization until you feel completely comfortable. Before you open your eyes and return to the real world, notice how you feel and ask yourself what you've learned about yourself and your tiny self. Assure yourself that Tiny You will be there when you present to a real audience. Once you feel the assurance, open your eyes. As you move once again in the real world, allow the effects of the visualization to stay with you.

Recreate this inner world as often as you need to. Let it become as real for you as the outer world. When your inner world is real enough to live side-by-side with your outer world, you will find it much easier to replace fear, anxiety, negativity, and resentment with flexibility and openness.

As you work now *with* your emotions, you will find yourself becoming excited where you once felt fearful. As you begin to develop a relationship with the Tiny You who is always present, you will gain enormous insight into yourself and your presentation. Learn to trust the insight and depend upon it. A strong connection with yourself helps to build your self confidence, personal comfort, and self-esteem, all of which are integral to turning fear into excitement.

9

Allow The Unique You To Emerge

Frank was an aspiring attorney who stopped growing as a human being after he entered law school. Slowly but steadily he learned to bury human emotions and reactions. These, he felt, hampered the development of the detail-oriented, calculating mind that he felt he needed to counter legal argument with legal argument and precedent with precedent. Even his wife, who had supported him emotionally through law school, now complained that he didn't listen to her and that he no longer was capable of a genuine discussion. Frank had become the lawyer that his legal training had regretably prepared him to be.

Klaus was an architect who dreamed of uniting form and function only to find that the world wasn't ready or willing to embrace his ideas. Once enthusiastic and optimistic, if a bit egotistic, Klaus became simply egocentric. He clung to his ego in the belief that he was protecting his dream. He battled for contracts from people he didn't respect and anguished over the constraints they put on his vision. He spent more and more time doing less and less rewarding work. He learned to expect resistance, and he generally got what he expected.

Corinne was a professional woman who resented that she was expected to be a nurturer simply because she was a woman. In reaction, she demanded more of others than did the men in her office, just because everyone expected her to be otherwise. She anguished over every natural human emotion, questioning and reevaluating every feeling until she found herself treating her husband and family the same way she treated her colleagues.

Beverly entered the workforce for the first time at the age of forty. She was mature and experienced in life, but she received only rejection from her younger associates. In order to cope, she conformed as much as possible to those around her—all the while battling a shrinking self-esteem and questioning her life choices.

All these people shared one thing in common. They were living lies, and they knew it. Each had stepped outside his or her own individuality and married an image. But the image proved to be different from what each expected or wanted it to be. They ended up confused. *I don't fit in. This isn't me. I should be more this way or less that way. What's wrong with me? Who am I?*

Find Your Unique Vision

There is nothing wrong with using an image for inspiration. But so often we end up selling our souls to it. As soon as we do this, we stop seeing ourselves as individuals. We give away our separate, unique selves and lose the ability to present ourselves as the individuals we are. We leave behind our truths and our unique gifts when we choose to carry the baggage of an image.

An image is an oversimplification. When we become enslaved to an image, we devalue all that is unique in ourselves in a futile effort to replace the individual with the recognizable and predictable; we make ourselves 'just like' everyone else who seems to embody the image. Cultivating these similarities may satisfy the need to belong. But, if we fail to recognize our differences or if we conceal our unique qualities in the name of being like someone else, we destroy our intimacy with ourselves. We end up having nothing to offer. Our pursuit of the image ends up making its attainment impossible. We need to find our unique vision if we ever hope to have the world listen to what we have to say.

We have been developing our identities and our presentation styles since birth, if not before. Many of us, however, have buried who we are under debris from the past, under outmoded assumptions about who we think we should be, under the expectations of others, and under the beliefs we hold about ourselves. Whether we are high-powered professionals facing career situations or mere mortals dealing with everyday routines, we will present ourselves much more effectively and clearly if we do so as ourselves and not as some fictional, unrealistic, or unattainable image. This chapter will help you clear away any useless, outmoded, or unnecessary baggage you might be carrying so that you can let the real you show itself.

Exploring Yourself

The real you is actually a complex thing. You have many sides. You may not even be aware of all the facets of your personality. To display yourselves honestly, it will help to know yourself as fully as you can.

The following exercise will help you understand who you are. Take as much time as you need to complete it. You may find that you aren't sure of all the answers. If this is the case, take as long as you need to answer the troubling questions. These are the answers that will be the most informative. The goal is discovery...and honesty. You don't have to share your answers with anyone but yourself. But if you can't be honest with yourself, then you may well still be married to that image.

Exercise: A "Real You" Inventory

The list below is composed of statements which may or may not describe you. Rate each statement by the extent to which it fits you according to the criteria below, and circle the appropriate letter in front of each statement according to the following key:

T - The statement is true now.
P - It was true in the past.
D - I am trying to develop this trait right now.
N - It is not true now, never was, and never will be.
C - I feel comfortable when I see this trait in myself or others.
O - I feel neither comfortable nor uncomfortable with the trait.
X - I feel uncomfortable with the trait.

T P D N / C O X   I have inner strength.
T P D N / C O X   I am a good leader.
T P D N / C O X   I am a good administrator.
T P D N / C O X   I have strong personal needs and desires.
T P D N / C O X   I am self-centered.
T P D N / C O X   I am dominating.
T P D N / C O X   I am egotistical.
T P D N / C O X   I am dependent upon others.
T P D N / C O X   I am sensitive to the feelings of others.
T P D N / C O X   I am cooperative.
T P D N / C O X   I enjoy detailed work.
T P D N / C O X   I am a good friend.
T P D N / C O X   I'd rather deny myself so that another can benefit.
T P D N / C O X   I'd rather be the leader than part of the group.
T P D N / C O X   I'm an adequate leader but not a dynamic one.
T P D N / C O X   I confuse others when I clarify myself and I don't know why.
T P D N / C O X   I am shy and don't contribute to group discussions.
T P D N / C O X   I am warm and friendly.
T P D N / C O X   I am very social.
T P D N / C O X   I am a good conversationalist.
T P D N / C O X   People enjoy listening to me.
T P D N / C O X   I am a good listener.

T P D N / C O X   I speak well.

T P D N / C O X   I write well.

T P D N / C O X   I scatter my energy.

T P D N / C O X   I am uncomfortable in social situations.

T P D N / C O X   I was a late bloomer.

T P D N / C O X   I am practical.

T P D N / C O X   I easily bring order out of disorganized things.

T P D N / C O X   I work long and hard.

T P D N / C O X   I am conscientious.

T P D N / C O X   I prefer difficult tasks to simple tasks.

T P D N / C O X   I am serious.

T P D N / C O X   I have strong likes and dislikes.

T P D N / C O X   I make strong distinctions between what is right and what is wrong.

T P D N / C O X   I am courageous.

T P D N / C O X   I am stubborn.

T P D N / C O X   I am rigid.

T P D N / C O X   I am frustrated by limits.

T P D N / C O X   I am disorganized and irresponsible.

T P D N / C O X   I am versatile.

T P D N / C O X   I can accomplish anything I want to.

T P D N / C O X   I am restless and impatient.

T P D N / C O X   It is difficult to finish a task.

T P D N / C O X   I enjoy change.

T P D N / C O X   I love to travel.

T P D N / C O X   I am enthusiastic.

T P D N / C O X   I am excited by my life.

T P D N / C O X   I am overwhelmed by opportunities.

T P D N / C O X   I am responsible.

T P D N / C O X   I am always ready to help.

T P D N / C O X   I am generous.

T P D N / C O X   I am an excellent teacher.

T P D N / C O X   I create balance.

T P D N / C O X   Others come to me for help.

T P D N / C O X   Family and friends are important to me.

T P D N / C O X   I am emotional.

T P D N / C O X   I am critical of myself and others.

T P D N / C O X   I am a perfectionist.

T P D N / C O X   Family and friends depend on me.

T P D N / C O X   I am different from others.

T P D N / C O X   I am introspective.

T P D N / C O X   I am reserved.

T P D N / C O X   I don't trust others.

T P D N / C O X   I don't adapt well.

T P D N / C O X   I prefer to be alone.

T P D N / C O X   I turn inward for answers.

T P D N / C O X   I am intuitive.

T P D N / C O X   I am not materialistic.

T P D N / C O X   I am ambitious.

T P D N / C O X   I am self-confident.

T P D N / C O X   I take charge and give direction.

T P D N / C O X   I am a good judge of character.

T P D N / C O X   I am realistic and practical.

T P D N / C O X   I am intolerant of others.

T P D N / C O X   I am the focus of resentment and hostility.

T P D N / C O X   I have difficulty seeing the forest because of the trees.

T P D N / C O X   I don't have the self-confidence to assert myself.

T P D N / C O X   I am interested in others.

T P D N / C O X   I am sympathetic, tolerant, and broadminded.

T P D N / C O X   I am disappointed by imperfection in the world.

T P D N / C O X   I am romantic.

T P D N / C O X   I am very imaginative.

T P D N / C O X   I am often dissatisfied.

T P D N / C O X   I am satisfied by giving.

Analyze The Results

First, look at those statements which you feel are true for you and which you also feel comfortable with. Do you use those traits to communicate effectively with others? If not, would you feel comfortable using those traits in your communication? If not, why? Are there any traits that you might use even more effectively?

Now look at the statements that you feel are true for you but you are uncomfortable with. How long have you had these traits? Do you remember how you acquired them? Is this ever a useful trait? Would you be better off by eliminating this trait or by minimizing it?

You wouldn't be normal if you weren't uncomfortable with at least a few traits. The above exercise was designed in part to help you bring these areas more prominently into your consciousness. Once you have identified these areas, you can make intentional and conscious efforts to do something about them, bringing about changes to your real self and not to the superficial veneer of some idealistic image.

Your conscious effort and awareness will do much to bring about these changes. You can speed the move in that direction by practicing one of the following techniques to eliminate undesirable characteristics.

Burn It: Write a complete description of the trait you wish to eliminate. Read the description over and make as many changes to your written description until you feel it describes the trait precisely.

Now burn the paper. As you watch it burn, say "I release (whatever the trait is) into the ethers." Imagine that the trait really is evaporating and diffusing harmlessly and gently into the air.

Draw A Family Tree: Trace the origins of this trait back in your family as far as you can. Who else in your life has this trait? How do you feel about that person? How did you feel when that person displayed the trait toward you? Was this trait ever useful, or has it always been an impediment? Help yourself eliminate the trait by imagining that you are asking the other person to change. How are you making the request? What exactly are you asking the person to do?

Communicate with your inner self: Ask Tiny You to display the uncomfortable trait visually so you can actually see it within yourself. How do you feel while watching it? What trait would you rather see in yourself? Now ask your inner self to show you the preferred trait? How do you feel now? Ask your inner self to replace the old trait with the new one. Visualize that you now possess the new trait.

Putting The Puzzle Together

You have looked at the pieces of your puzzle. Now, it is time to put them together again. As you go through the process, you will become better able to focus your intention sharply and to make your intention and your personal self work more as one. You will have a better sense of where you want to go and how you can actually get there. The image you project will become an authentic one and not a charicature of what can never be.

Using everything you have learned about yourself, write down a description of the you that you want to be. Include the traits you are developing and those you would like to develop as well as the traits you already exhibit. Take as long as you need to describe the ideal you, and revise your description whenever it needs to be revised. Read your description often and as you read, visualize the person you are describing until you get a clear picture of yourself as you want to be.

Now refine your description down to a single sentence. Memorize it. Turn it into an affirmation, a positive statement affirming that you already are what you are trying to become: *I am a powerful, compassionate, and articulate speaker*, for example.

Let your affirmation direct your attention toward your goal. Repeat it aloud several times per day—when you wake up, when you look into the mirror, when you get dressed and undressed, when you leave your home, when you begin work, when you come home, when you go to sleep at night, and any time when you feel afraid, threatened, angry, or off-balance. Each time you repeat your affirmation, see it as if it were already real, feel it, do whatever you can to believe that it is a description of the real you. Consider your affirmation as your guiding star, pointing the way toward your destination to keep you on course and to bring you back on course when you stray.

Acknowledge Your Tools

Your personal style brings together everything you are and everything you want to be. It is an expression of the real you. Anything else is a false front. Finding your personal style means accepting yourself as you are right now. You can't fool yourself into becoming something you are not, and you can't fool others, either. To be authentic and credible to others, you need to be authentic and credible to yourself.

Accepting yourself for yourself gives you a foundation on which to build. The real you is always changing and evolving. Its starting point is right now. Understanding who you are today allows you to know what you need to do to become who you want to be, because it allows you to understand where you are starting and what you have to work with. You need to understand and appreciate your unique strengths and weaknesses, both to plot your future course and to make the most of the tools you currently possess.

10

Turning On
Your Inner Voice

The first chapters of this book introduced some technical and personal skills you can use to prepare your body, voice, and imagination for making effective, willful presentations. To make full use of these technical skills, however, you need something more. You also need inspiration—that combination of skill, intention, and trust that makes communication bloom. This sounds simple, but in reality it is perhaps the most challenging and paradoxical presentation skill you will learn.

Inspiration cannot be practiced. It comes from quietness, trust, and faith. Quietness lets you hear your inspiration talking. Trust in your own intimate knowledge of your abilities—your inner knowing—frees your inspiration to soar. Faith that your inspiration is true silences the doubts and fears that so often stand in the way.

Quiet Your Mind

To be inspired, you must first learn how to silence your mind so you can open it to hear. You have to give up control in order to listen. You have to be focussed so your quiet mind can hear.

Think about a time when you were truly inspired. Perhaps your inspiration appeared as a flash of insight from the outside. Perhaps it grew out of a deep inner knowing. Whatever its source, your inspiration was possible because your mind was open to receive it. Your mind had to set aside judging long enough to be open and receptive.

Unfortunately, most of us spend very little time in this state of openness. Instead, we chatter about and comment on life's experiences. The mind can be a pathway to inspiration, or it can be the greatest barrier to it. Much of our task is learning how to tell our minds to shut up and get out of the way.

We can take a hint from the discipline of meditation. A quote on the wall of one meditation studio in my neighborhood reads: "I meditate to not let my mind complicate my life." Meditation is a technique of quieting the mind so that intention and inner voice can assert themselves. A chattering mind, a condemning mind, an interfering mind, a mind that judges everything we do and comments on all our actions—this mind complicates life. This meddling mind stifles our inner knowing and second-guesses our instincts. Meditation teaches us to quiet the chatter and allow the inner voice to fill the void.

To Lead, Give Up

Margo built her successful business through public speaking engagements. She had worked hard to become so clear about her intention that she would be able to hear the unvoiced questions from her audience and respond intuitively. "It's happening!" she told me recently. "I can hear the needs of my audience!" But, she still had misgivings. "Now that I'm actually hearing, I am not sure what to do about it."

The only advice I could give her was to trust that her intuition and her natural knowing would guide her words to the right response for her audience. She had developed her technique. She heard the audience's unspoken desires. Now she needed to let go of the doubts and to trust herself.

Margo understood immediately. "You mean that I should stop trying to control the situation with my agenda and my need to convey certain information, right?" Her years of experience made the next step obvious. "If I trust myself and my audience, my loss of control will actually improve my communication because I will be addressing the needs of my audience and not my own personal needs. Ultimately I will have greater influence and control."

Margo realized something that can never be taught. It can only be learned through first-hand experience. The way to lead is to follow. The way to communicate is to listen. The way to succeed is to trust that success will happen and get out of the way.

Spontaneity And Personal Freedom

Actors open the door to inspiration by learning how to improvise, to create something from nothing. Viola Spolin, the grandmother of improvisation and theatre games, calls improvisation a form of spontaneity, a "personal freedom" that can be enjoyed when we see reality for what it is. Only when we interact with what simply is can we explore reality and act appropriately. To do this, we need to let go and trust ourselves and our abilities.

Improvisation training helps actors remove the walls around inspiration. It takes away *no, I can't,* and *never* and replaces them with *yes, I can,* and *always*. Practicing improvisation helps actors discover and eliminate the mental, emotional, and physical blocks to expression. As each block is removed, an explosion of creativity emerges. Layers of creative expression are stored just on the other side of consciousness, waiting to be released. What releases them is abandoning the effort to control. Control is nothing more than resistance—resistance to listening, resistance to feeling, resistance to experiencing the sights, sounds, and feelings in the world around us. Improvisation, by contrast, is a response to the feelings, sights, and sounds that control keeps us from experiencing.

Never Say No

I introduce improvisation to my clients with a game called *Never Say No*. Two people participate. They pretend to be at a bus stop waiting for a bus to take them to the places of their choosing.

The point of the game is to engage in a bus-stop conversation without using words that stop communication—words like *no, not, never, can't, won't, shouldn't,* and *couldn't.* In addition, each player must continually add to the communication. Whenever a player uses a forbidden word, I ask for a correction by interrupting, "You what?" The player makes the correction and moves on. The game generally proceeds something like this.

(First player) Hi, have you been at this bus stop before?
(Second player) No, I haven't.
(I interrupt) You what?
Do I have to say, "yes, I have been here?"
Find another way to communicate your meaning.
Actually, this is my first time at this bus stop.
Now add something to the communication.
I've just moved into the area.
So you don't know where to go?
You what?
So, you need help finding your bus. Well, this map may be useful. Here take a look.
Well, actually, my eye sight isn't...I mean, I can't...I mean, would you please read the map for me?
I'd be glad to. Just where do you want to go?
Poughkeepsie.
You can't get there...I mean, you'll need to get on a bus to the main terminal—that's Number 3, which I see coming right now. When you get to the terminal ask someone for directions.
Thanks for everything. I couldn't have...I mean, I was lost without your help.

Never Say No brings several important concepts to the surface. Most of us respond to new situations and new people by putting up walls that block communication. We separate ourselves by finding differences instead of blending with others and finding similarities. Often, this separation blocks communication and makes everyone feel awkward and uncomfortable.

When we eliminate words that block and replace them with descriptive images, communication opens up and the wall vanishes. As the communication wall is lifted, other walls disappear as well. Communication becomes relaxed and free of emotional pressure. The focus shifts from self to the needs of the other. Inspiration can enter the dialogue and guide the communication. Communication becomes a dance instead of a head-butting contest.

Technique And Inspiration

For centuries, people just *knew* that certain things were true. We would never travel faster than a horse could travel, never fly, never set foot on another body in the solar system. Albert Einstein's teachers knew that he would never amount to anything. Roger Bannister knew that no one would ever run a four-minute mile. Even today, many of us 'know' that a woman will never be President and that we will never find a cure for the common cold.

Inspiration, by contrast, does not accept the limits such common wisdom imposes. Common wisdom is negative, serving as a blinder on vision. It tells us what can't be. Inspiration tells us what might be. Inspiration doesn't care about what is 'impossible.' Instead, it fixes its gaze on the boundary between what is possible and what can be imagined. The inspired person seems like a visionary; the uninspired person seems like a slug.

You can't be inspired without also being motivated. It is possible to be motivated without also being inspired, but it is impossible to *stay* motivated without being inspired. On the other hand, it is impossible to be inspired without becoming motivated, for true inspiration creates its own motivation.

Inspiration keeps our feet on the ground. It is not just a product of fantasy. What keeps inspiration rooted is technique. Technique is the ballast that ties imagination to experience. Technique is what we have done and what we have learned is possible to do. Technique is the key to performance. To the untrained, technique is a mystery; to those who have mastered the skill, technique is an old, familiar friend.

Inspiration also comes from confidence. Studying and mastering technique enhances the self-esteem and self-assurance of the presenter. To those who know that they have accomplished the mastery of technique comes a sense of self-empowerment, an *I can* understanding of who they are and what they can do. This is often the quiet confidence that shows itself by its actions more than its words.

The Different Forms of Inspiration

Inspiration arrives in many forms. Sometimes it takes the form of actual words. At other times, it appears as an image, a feeling, or a hunch. It can seem to be the result of pure coincidence or accident. It may seem like a mystical revelation, an empirical insight, or a profound *aha!* experience.

However you receive your inspiration or insight, you will be much more receptive to it if you are prepared to receive it. That nagging feeling could be your subconscious telling you that it has figured it all out before your conscious has. That instinct or insight could be the spontaneous, unspoken product of all the planning you have done. That gut-level intuition could be the natural outgrowth of knowing what you are doing or what you are talking about.

Never be afraid to ask for inspiration. Whether you ask your subconscious, the universe, or a higher power, the very act of asking for direction invites inspiration to enter. Asking sets the process in motion. It makes you ready to hear what inspiration can tell you. It defines what the problem is and where the solution may lie. It focusses your own attention on getting from here to there. It reaffirms your own motivation to be inspired.

I teach my clients the following technique for inviting inspiration. Sit comfortably and take a slow, deep breath or two. Ask for help, either silently or aloud, as if you were speaking to a friend. *Please help me understand what I need to do to... Please give me the words which will... Please give me insight into...* Expect to get an answer, if not right away then as soon as it is time for the answer to appear. Take a few more slow, deep breaths. When the inspiration does come—and this is important—act on it.

Be open to receiving the inspiration in whatever form it may take. It may not always arrive in the way you expect. One client, for example, found her inspiration in a series of very mundane, everyday coincidences. For years Gloria's close friends had simply called her by her initials, G.L. Several years ago, Gloria had to decide about one of her long-cherished career goals. Did she really have the ability to do what she had been dreaming of doing, or should she give up her dreams and follow a safer, more traditional path? Was she willing to put out the effort, planning, and persistence into her project, or was she just kidding herself?

During the two or three months while she was contemplated her decision, Gloria noticed that she was constantly driving, parking, or stopping behind Hyundai EXCEL GL™ models. She considered this to be a message, a vote of confidence in her abilities and a reminder that she had grown beyond her youthful limitations. Gloria realized that this could have been nothing more than a coincidence. But the message seemed to answer the question she was asking, so she listened.

There was more. Gloria embarked on her project only to discover that she needed financial help to make it happen. Shortly after she had completed these financial projections, a friend called to ask Gloria to accompany her on a visit to a mutual friend. Gloria could have found many reasons not to go. But she asked for guidance, and something said, "Go." While on this trip, Gloria met the investor who would make her project possible. Again, this may have been a coincidence. But you will never convince Gloria that her intention, her inspiration, her motivation, and her technique didn't somehow work in unison to make it happen.

Inspiration: The Result Of Great Technique.

What may seem like an accident, a coincidence, or even a miracle is actually anything but. Inspiration doesn't just happen. It is the fruit of the careful cultivation of technique. The farmland must be plowed, planted, watered, and tended before the crop will grow. Technique must be developed and practiced before inspiration can find its expression.

Do not ignore the development of technique. Blind inspiration without the focus of technique can only lead to ungrounded, non-specific actions without a real purpose. True inspiration, which springs from a carefully conceived intention, a clearly defined vision, and a faith in techniques already learned, is the final ingredient for turning ordinary communication into extraordinary presentation.

11

Getting Comfortable With Your Audience

Your successful presentation will depend in part on your ability to reach out and touch the individual members of your audience emotionally. This act of reaching out forms a reciprocal bond between you and those whom you are speaking to. It makes a connection that virtually obliges your audience to care about you and what you are saying, because it helps them feel your concern for them and what they want. When you are connected with your audience, you share a comfort and an intimacy that includes everyone in a common experience. The result is a much more powerful and effective presentation.

Successful actors have learned to build this intimacy by expanding and sharing their 'personal space.' We all have a personal space, a physical and emotional area where we feel capable of acting independently and effectively. The typical understanding of personal space is the so called 'comfort zone' that marks the boundaries of our personal territory. Here in North America, we usually consider our comfort zone to be the area eighteen or twenty inches around us. Let a stranger or a casual acquaintance enter this space, and we feel uncomfortable, threatened, or self-conscious. Let a lover or a mate enter the space, and we feel affectionate and connected.

Personal space is actually much more than this comfort zone. It is an emotional, psychological, even psychic domain where our interactions with others are mutual. It is more a thing you can feel than a thing you can measure, but it is nonetheless an important and very real dimension of our presentation skills. Personal space may be difficult to define, but it is not difficult to recognize.

Remember a time when you became so involved with another person that time seemed to fly by? Remember a time when you and another person hit it right off and a camaraderie appeared spontaneously? Remember a time when you were in total command of a situation and rose to every occasion naturally and spontaneously?

In each of these situations, you experienced not just personal space, but the sharing of personal space. What made things click was that you were sharing more than a mere physical presence. You were 'on the same wavelength' in part because, consciously or not, you chose to expand your personal space far enough to include the others who needed to be included.

This chapter discusses how you can turn your personal space into part of your presentation. Whether you are speaking to a single other or to an audience full of strangers, you will find that being able to include others in your personal space becomes one of your presentation tools.

Commitment And Personal Space

A meeting between you and another person or between you and a group is a mutual discovery that requires complete, mutual commitment. Each of you must be willing to open your personal spaces to the other for the duration of the presentation if you expect to enjoy a shared experience. You cannot force others to open their spaces to you, but you can invite them to and make it easy for them to open themselves up to what you are saying.

To open your personal space, you must do two things. First, you need to become comfortable in the presence of others. You do this by choosing to feel the presence of another without feeling threatened. Second, you need to let your comfort expand to include the other. This establishes a intangible connection between you and your audience, one you can continue to feel even at a distance.

When the communication is over, you must reclaim your personal space, recharge your energy, and stand back to look at the whole picture. During this recharge time, let your subconscious take over. Just as your subconscious helps you solve problems when you 'sleep on it' or when you simply sit back and 'put it out of your mind,' your subconscious will help you understand what you need to understand. But you have to get out of its way so it can work unhampered. You may not be able to stop in mid-presentation to make uninterrupted room for your subconscious to work, but you can learn to be more sensitive to what your subconscious is telling you.

This expansion of personal space can be intoxicating. However, always remember that, when you invite others into your personal space, you are inviting them 'as is.' They bring with them all the baggage they carry around with them, all their hopes, fears, anxieties, and feelings. These can be overwhelming if you do not close your personal space back down when you are done. If you retain the baggage of others, you will not be able to let your subconscious run free. Your effectiveness, your peace of mind, and perhaps even your health will suffer.

Expanding Your Personal Space

One of the most effective ways to expand your personal space is to recognize exactly how far you have to expand it. Usually, this is only far enough to include your audience. Before you begin speaking, make eye contact with the people seated at the outer perimeter of your audience. Make sure that you see their eyes and that they see yours. This is important—it becomes an invitation for them to join you during the presentation.

Practice this technique in your home or office by substituting pieces of furniture, books, or walls for people.

After you define the perimeter with your eyes, practice your presentation while continuing to make eye contact with these surrogate people within your practice boundaries. This practice will help you turn the process into a natural and unselfconscious one.

On your actual speaking day, find an opportunity to make eye contact with the audience boundaries before you get up to present. (This is particularly easy if you are sitting on stage waiting to speak). When you stand to make your presentation, refresh your mind by quickly making eye contact with the people at the extremes of your audience. With practice, you will naturally find their eyes several more times during the course of your presentation.

Seeing the limits of your audience gives your subconscious mind the information it needs to expand your personal space to the appropriate size. Your subconscious can now guide your mind in making your gestures large enough and your voice loud enough to keep your audience involved.

As you learn how to expand your personal space sufficiently, your audiences will feel closer and more comfortable with you. They will be encouraged to relax and extend their openness to you in return. When your audience is comfortable and open, they will be more willing to concentrate on and listen to every word you say. In fact, you may even notice emotional bonds forming among audience members. Two or more people seated near each other, for example, may begin to respond in unison. When this happens, you will know that your audience is indeed sharing a group experience.

Meanwhile, you will find that the energy of your audience nourishes your presentation. Once you have included your audience in your personal space, their energy is concentrated on one individual—you, the speaker, the person they have come to hear. Feel this energy, accept it, and use it to heighten your performance even further. Let the communication become a partnership between you and your audience.

Concentrate The Energy

Theatre offers techniques to amplify this sharing of energy. One of the most widely known tricks is to make the house appear to be full. Theater managers know that a full theater generally creates a better experience for both actor and audience than a half-full house. But 'full' is a relative term. In order to make a house seem full, some managers will physically remove unsold seats. Others give out free tickets to ensure that all the seats are filled. These managers understand that an empty seat is a vacuum for energy between actor and audience. By removing seats or filling them with non-paying theater-goers, managers can amplify the energy of a performance.

Many actors notice the difference. They can feel the energy of an audience, and they can have very difficult times when houses are less than full. It is not that they feel an empty seat is a mark of rejection. For many, a performance requires a lot more work when there are empty seats, simply because the actor is not being re-energized by the attention and participation of the audience.

During your presentation, try to ensure that you are speaking to as full a house as possible. If you have some control over the physical accommodations, plan to have just enough seats or reserve a room that is just the right size. Even if you cannot influence the logistics, you can still encourage the audience to move toward the center when you begin your presentation. Anything you can do to fill the house or eliminate empty spaces will have a major influence on the effectiveness of your presentation.

One-On-One Presentations

Speaking to a single person involves the same techniques plus a few person-to-person skills. In the abstract, one-on-one communication involves the meeting of equals. In the real world, however, one-on-one communication is often between people who are not equal. More often than not, one person needs something that the other can provide. This can change the dynamics of the presentation.

If you need the help, for example, you may be tempted to keep your personal space compact and your energy contained. Yielding to this temptation could be a mistake. Now is the time to relax and expand your personal space as far as you can so that your invitation to share the meeting can be understood. Closing down and making your space small can give the impression that you are not totally available and invite the other to stay at a safe distance.

If you have what is sought, you are in control. But that doesn't mean that you are free of responsibility. You are still presenting yourself, even if the other person has come to ask you for something. You are responsible for extending your personal space and creating a comfort zone for the exchange. A doctor who practices this way has good bedside manner. A shopkeeper who runs his business has customers who feel comfortable in his store. A psychiatrist who practices this way has clients who feel safe opening up.

Listen With Your Third Ear

Whether you are speaking to a large group or to a single person, it is important to listen and watch for clues to the feelings and attitude of your audience. Recall the discussion of listening with the mind and body in Chapter 3. You can also listen with your instincts.

As we have seen, communication may rely on words, but communication is far more than words alone. Communication is a complex interaction of words and word choices, word clusters, pauses, volumes, pitches, and paces. Reading between or behind the lines can often make an otherwise muddy meaning clear. Different word choices, for example, can convey very different messages. Consider the differences between *We have been as dedicated as necessary to this project, but we ran out of time.* and *We really tried to make this project a success, but we ran out of time.* Which of the two admissions of defeat feels more sincere?

Consider where pauses occur. What is the differences in meaning between *Are you saying that ... managers will have to supervise this training*? and *Are you saying that managers will have to ... supervise this training*? Combine this sensitivity to words with a sensitivity to emphasis: *Are you saying that **managers** will have to supervise this training? Are you saying that managers will have to **supervise** this training?*

Listen to the directness or indirectness with which the words flow. You learn something much different from a simple *No, thank you.* than from a much more convoluted *I've considered that but, to tell you the truth, and believe me this is important, I've thought about it a lot, I guess it just isn't for me, at least I don't think so.*

Consider the volume a person uses and when it changes. What would you conclude if someone told you *I'm interested in hearing more about this. **But, I don't quite believe what you're telling me?*** What is the difference between words said with vocal variety and words said in a monotone? What do you feel when someone attempts to inject humor into a question or a response? What is your response when someone throws a bunch of technical jargon at you?

How committed is the person who is speaking? Feel for clues in what the person says. *We believe that everyone who works in this department needs a computer* is much different from *The company attempts to provide a computer for everyone who needs one.* Does the person speaking use first person to own his or her own statements (*I do... I go...* or *I am...*), or does he or she speak in distance-producing generalizations (*You can't... You have to...* or *You don't want to...*).

What visual clues are your listener(s) sending you? Whether the person is speaking to you or listening to what you are saying, pay attention to way the person communicates. Observe the physical way in which a person speaks. Note the facial and physical gestures of a person who is listening. Mirror the words of the other as you learned to do in Chapter 3, making an effort to find a common 'wavelength.'

It is not just the speaker or the listener who is sending clues. Pay attention to the individuals sitting near the speaker, for example. There may be a group culture or a collective consciousness that you need to know about. Notice how they shift their posture or physical positions. Are they communicating agreement or disagreement? How many appear to agree with the statements or questions of the speaker? How do they respond to your answers? Be sensitive to shifts in attitude, physical positions, and concentration. If you feel it necessary or appropriate, acknowledge these shifts with a statement like *Some of you seem to disagree with me or not to understand what I just said. Is that an accurate read?*

As you speak, your audience will be answering in their movement, their concentration, their eye contact, and their general posture. Any changes that occur as you move from subject to subject will be telling you that something is going on in your listeners' minds. Notice everything. Judge nothing. Trust your intuition to recognize what is important.

It would be impossible to list all the nuances that go into even ordinary communication. Understanding these nuances means opening yourself up to a kind of communication that many of us don't think about all that often. Still, we can all cultivate this art of reading between the lines. It does take practice, as well as the courage to believe what your instincts are telling you, even when your ears are telling you something else. But once you have mastered this skill, you will find that you are able to hear what everyone within your personal space is saying, both in words and in meanings.

Achievement and Satisfaction

A comfortable presentation is a successful presentation. The more you are able to expand your personal space, share the energy, and listen intuitively, the better able you will be to make a successful presentation. How will you know that you have succeeded?

Actors always know how their performance went. *I really hit the moments tonight.... I had trouble getting to the big emotional breakdown in scene two, so I had to play it a little less intensely.... I started out too strong, so I really had to pull back before the climax.* These are typical responses you might hear backstage to the question, "How did you do tonight?"

You, too, will know how your presentation went. Your conscious mind will tell you how well you achieved your intentions. Your intuition will tell you how well you made contact with your audience. The response of your listeners will tell you how comfortably they were with what you were trying to say. And above all, your own satisfaction with your presentation will tell you how well you did tonight.

12

Keeping Your Audience Satisfied

Your presentation is all worked out, its details are specific, its information has been clarified. It seems complete. Once your presentation reaches this point, you may be tempted to present it exactly the same way time after time. There is a security in sameness. After all, it works, doesn't it?

This is an invitation to disaster. The danger is very real that your presentation will become a formula, a one-size-fits-all non-solution to sharing information. This is flirting with boredom, not communication. If your presentation is not specific to the time, place, and audience each time you give it, you are running the risk that it will not meet the unique needs or wants of your listeners. You need to make it fresh, even if you have made the same presentation everyday in recent memory.

You can't be expected to reinvent the presentation each time you address your audience. But you also cannot expect to give a dynamic presentation when you are bored. What you can do is add some 'planned spontaneity' to your presentation by finding out something about your audience and taking what you have learned into consideration each time you plan your presentation.

I learned this lesson, almost the hard way, when I was a member of a touring college theater. We spent one summer traveling around the state of Colorado, performing the same two plays over and over again in some of the smallest towns in the state. You can imagine how tedious this routine became. Within a few weeks, we had become very tired of doing the same two plays day in and day out.

It showed. We knew, from our own feelingsand from what we saw on the faces of the audiences, that we were heading for trouble. Then one member of the company began to incorporate local color into his performance. He used the name of the town's football rival when he was talking about evil. He learned the names of the local political leaders and made up bits of information about them. We all joined in. We used the name of the town in the play. We made reference to local history and local lore. If there was a particular landmark in the region, it would end up somewhere in the play. We found a way to put on each performance *As If* we were putting it on for the first time.

We noticed the results right away. Our audiences were more involved with our performances. They paid more attention during the performance and they left the theater with bigger smiles and brighter eyes. It meant only a little extra work for us, sometimes as little as a ten or fifteen minute discussion with one or two local residents. The plays remained essentially the same except for our occasional use of 'planned spontaneity.'

Know Your Audience

To make an effective presentation, you need to know who you are talking to. This means doing some research and finding out everything you can about your audience. How much do they know about your subject, for example? How much do they want or need to know? Why don't they already know it? Is there any information that is unique to the individuals or the industry you are speaking to?

It is easy to include your audience in the stories you tell or the examples you give. If you don't, you run the risk of losing your audience to boredom or disinterest. Consider what happened at a recent conference for attorneys. More than half the audience was female, but the mostly male presenters consistently referred to judges as *he* and in other ways appeared to be talking to less than half the audience. This did not go unnoticed. Post-conference evaluations reflected the audiences' disappointment in the lack of reference to female role models. This disappointment could have been avoided easily if the speakers had taken a little time to find out who they were talking to.

Knowing your audience helps you persuade your audience and makes listeners more receptive to what you are saying. This act of involving your audience also helps you stay spontaneous, because it means you are actively involved in the presentation. By treating each audience as the unique body that it is, you will become more involved in your audience and your message and more likely to respond when inspiration calls.

Making It Spontaneous

Remember that audiences listen with more than their ears. They translate your words and actions into something meaningful for them. Something you say may evoke a visual image for one person, an emotion for another, a memory for a third. You can't control the precise reaction of each audience member, but that doesn't matter. What matters is that the audience members do relate to your presentation.

One way to ensure this is to make sure that you relate to your presentation. Review the discussion on "Presenting *As If*" in Chapter 5. Make your presentation real for yourself and for your listeners by seeing, hearing, and feeling the images you speak about through the eyes, ears, and emotions of your audience.

Another way to add spontaneity to your presentation is to leave room for questions or discussions during or after your presentation. Make sure your audience knows that they will have an opportunity to ask their own questions or make their own comments. Not only will this communicate your desire to speak to your listeners' concerns, but it will also encourage the audience to pay attention during your presentation. Almost by definition, questions and comments add newness and spontaneity to your presentation. Finally, questions and comments give you yet another opportunity to assess the needs of your audience and tailor your responses to meet those needs.

Audience members will frequently ask questions that go beyond the relatively specific meaning of their words. As we have seen, finding the meaning behind a questioner's words will help you answer the question and address the concerns that lie behind the question. Recognizing the question behind the question is a skill that comes with practice. It is a lot easier to learn if you keep in mind some of the skills we have already talked about: be clear about your intention, be able to listen empathetically, and be open to reading between and behind the lines.

Sometimes a questioner is motivated by something as simple as a desire for you to confirm that what he or she is already doing is appropriate. At other times, a comment or question will be a sign that something is going on under the surface—a power struggle, perhaps, or some other undisclosed distraction. Even if the question or comment seems to be contrary or provocative for no particular reason, that very fact gives you additional information about what is going on behind the scenes.

The background question may reflect the concerns of the individual who is asking the question or making the comment. But it may also reflect a common concern among the entire group. Notice the reactions of others in the audience—does there seem to be a general agreement among the listeners? If so, acknowledge the question and use this new information as a opportunity to learn more about common concerns of your audience. A simple way to do this is to ask a follow-up question of your own. A response like *That is a very good question. Has anyone else had a similar experience?* can help you establish a rapport with your audience and make your point at the same time.

After you have made the same presentation several times, you may find the questions become similar from one talk to the next. This makes finding newness and spontaneity an even greater challenge, because you may begin thinking that you already know what the questioner is thinking. You my even be tempted to finish the question for the person asking it.

Don't yield to this temptation. Even if you are right—even if you *have* heard the question before—the questioner has not asked the question before. And if you are wrong—if you have interrrupted the questioner to finish a question *not* being asked—you will have cut off an opportunity to involve your audience in your presentation. So, curb your impulse and, instead, listen to the question *as if for the first time.* By showing genuine interest, you are more likely to hear the real concern behind the question. Your questioner will more likely be satisfied that the question was indeed heard and acknowledged.

A satisfied audience is an involved audience. And an involved audience will be much more receptive to your message and much more likely to share your presentation. Whatever you can do to encourage audience involvement and participation will pay off in a more productive and more satisfying presentation, both for your audience and for you.

13

Intentions, Goals, and Personal Power

Dynamic presentations are natural to those who have the personal power that comes from a balanced life. When you have personal power, things work without extra effort, and the successes you experience in one part of your life make successes in other parts easier to achieve. Personal power is not the raw power that is associated with aggression, manipulation, or violence. That is nothing more than force. True personal power is the ability to live so that all parts of your life work smoothly together. Presentation skills are natural extensions of personal power.

Real, personal power comes from the confidence that accompanies clear intentions and achievable goals. Personal power is not created out of thin air. It is a natural and inevitable by-product of all that we have learned so far. Personal power is magnetic, effortlessly attracting to itself the practical results that so many people labor self-consciously to achieve. Personal power is more than charisma; it has as much to do with internal harmony and clarity as it does with external appearances.

The path to personal power starts when we begin asking who we are and who we want be. Many people find these some of the most difficult questions to answer, because the answers touch on some of the most sensitive and personal parts of our lives. But answer them we must, unless we are content to follow the hazards of fate or the expectations of others. Defining who we want to be puts us well down the road to being who we want to be. The first step in the process is to examine our intentions and goals.

Goals, Intentions, and Action Steps

Goals and intentions are complementary sides of the same question. An intention is a generalization. It is a description of a quality or attribute of life that we want to achieve. You might, for example, want to be a dynamic speaker or a successful attorney. You might want to create a closely-knit company of trusting, talented employees. You might want to be a dutiful niece or nephew to your Aunt Millie in Poughkeepsie. An intention is a general destination that tells you where you want to go, stated as if you are already there.

If the intention is your destination, your goals are your map. Goals need to be stated in measurable terms so you can use them as yardsticks to judge your progress. As part of your duty to Aunt Millie, your goal might be to get from White Plains to Poughkeepsie by four on Tuesday afternoon.

Action steps are the specific things you will do to accomplish your goals. These are concrete steps which you can point to, schedule, or do. In the above example, to get to Poughkeepsie on time, you may identify the following action steps: leave work at two; put regular-grade gas in the car; follow highway 287 to the Taconic Parkway; go north on the Taconic to route 55; then take route 55 into Poughkeepsie and Aunt Millie's house.

The more clearly you define your intentions, the more suitable your goals will be. Clearly stated intentions point toward clearly measurable and appropriate goals. Together, your goals and intentions create the results you desire. If your intentions are ambiguous, your goals may be inappropriate. If you define your intentions without staking out your goals, you will have no plan for accomplishment.

The following exercise is based on the well-known process of 'goal setting.' It will help you clarify your intentions and your goals. Work through it carefully, taking as much time as you need to do it thoroughly. It may take days or even weeks to complete. So be it. The benefits you stand to gain are certainly worth the relatively small amount of time the exercise takes.

When you are done, you will have a snapshot of where you stand right now. Don't hesitate to rethink your intentions or your goals whenever you feel it is appropriate. Expect your goals and intentions to change constantly as your life moves forward. If your intentions change or your goals get out of harmony with your intentions, acknowledge this and revise your plans accordingly.

Redo the exercise periodically to make sure that your destination is still the place where you want to go.

Exercise: Defining Intentions, Goals, and Action Steps

Identify those categories of life which are most important to you. Don't feel you have to confine your list to presentation or professional concerns. Your life cannot be broken down into some arbitrary collection of personal or professional compartments. Your list of categories should contain all the parts of your life that are meaningful to you. I recommend that you include at least the following categories: *personal, financial, family, spiritual, career, mental,* and *physical,* but do feel free to revise these categories to fit your own priorities. Take a separate piece of paper for each category and write the category on the top line.

Analyze each category very carefully. Beginning with the first, identify your intentions for this area of your life. Take your time. List as many possible intentions as come to mind. When you have finished your list, look all of your possible intentions over and come up with a single statement that summarizes your overall intention for this part of your life. Restate this statement as a positive *I am* affirmation, such as *I am a powerful speaker whose words others are eager to hear*. This will help make the intention seem real and accessible and not just something you have yet to achieve.

Once you are satisfied that your intention statement accurately reflects your desires, begin to list your goals. These are the concrete, measurable results you expect to achieve en route to accomplishing each of your intentions. Your goals should harmonize with your intentions; the completion of a goal should automatically realize a step toward an intention.

Action steps are the specific things you will do to accomplish your goals. Once you have identified your goals, your action steps will tell you exactly how you are going achieve them. Your action steps tell you what to do first and what you have to do before you can complete a subsequent step. List all of the action steps you need to complete in order to achieve your goal, even if you have already completed the steps. This will allow you not only to gauge where you are in the entire process, but also to give yourself credit for what you have already accomplished.

When you have completed your listing of goals and action steps, you will have an outline of the path from where you are today to where you want to be tomorrow. Now you need to orchestrate your progress by scheduling each action step and goal. Examine each goal and each action step. Set realistic target dates for accomplishing each.

Be practical in your scheduling estimates. Some goals or action steps require that other goals or action steps be completed first or take specific amounts of time to achieve. You need to graduate law school before you can practice law, for example, or intern for so many years before you can practice medicine. Some things can only be done at certain times. Certain meetings, for example, are only held on specific days of the year.

Other goals or action steps depend on the cooperation of others. You get your building permit when you get it, and no sooner. Still others are beyond your control entirely. You cannot force the stock market to go up. Don't be overly ambitious about your plans to achieve each milestone quickly. But don't be excessively casual either. Both are invitations for disappointment.

When you have analyzed all of your goals and action \ steps, stand back and look at the the big picture. How realistic is the entire package? Are you getting in over your head by trying to do too much in too short a period? Are your goals and steps compatible? Are you scheduling a week-long vacation in the Rockies under one category at the same time as you are planning a gala party in Seattle under another? Can you combine some of the action steps so you can work toward more than a single goal at one time? Can you eliminate a goal or an action step from one category because you have accomplished an equivalent one in another?

Be prepared to do a certain amount of fine-tuning in order to make this process work. And be prepared, also, to review your plans from time to time to make sure you are still on schedule, to make necessary corrections, and to change direction if that is called for.

If corrections need to be made, make them. The real joy and reward from the process lies in bringing it to fruition. Don't let awkward planning rob you of this joy by making it impossible for you to accomplish what you really want to accomplish. The more successfully you pass each milestone, the more realistic your prospects of attaining your vision become.

An Example

Sidebar 13A on page 123 is a typical, completed planning page. Your planning page may or may not look like this, because you need to put it into a form that works for you. What this form illustrates is the way this process can actually create a roadmap for your progress.

Along the top of the form is the intention, stated in the form of an affirmation. Beneath the intention statement is a listing of goals and a sequence of action steps that should lead to the achievement of the goal.

Exercise: A Life In Balance

Balancing all of your intentions is the key to balancing your life. It will do you little good to put all of your energy into your career, for example, if you ignore your health, your family, or your peace of mind. If you have examined the intentions that truly are important to your life, it is a simple matter to measure how well your life is in balance.

Draw a large circle on a piece of paper. Draw as many lines from the center of the circle to the edge as you have intentions, spacing them evenly apart. Label each of these spokes with the name of one of your intentions.

Think about your current progress toward each of these intentions. Place a small x on each line at a point that corresponds with how close you are to achieving the intention. If you have made little progress, place your x near the center of the circle. If you are close to achieving the intention, place the x closer to the outer edge of the circle.

When each spoke has an x, connect all the points and examine the shape of the figure that you have just drawn. If it resembles a circle that crosses each spoke at about the same distance from the center, your life is in relative balance. On the other hand, if it dips or jags because a line or two crosses the spokes closer to the center or the edge, your figure is telling you not only that your life is imbalanced, but also which parts of your life need more attention.

Study the wheel also to learn more about yourself. Where are your strengths? Have you spent more time

Professional

I am a dynamic speaker whom everyone wants to listen to

Goals and Action Steps:

- By December 1, 19___ I have completed all preparations necessary to make my presentation
  - ✔ Read all product information and sales literature by February 1, 19___
  - ✔ Order business cards and stationery by February 1, 19___
  - ✔ Complete my presentation outline by April 15, 19___
  - ✔ Complete a presentation seminar by May 31, 19___
  - ✔ Sign up for presentation coaching by June 1, 19___
  - ✔ Finish scripting presentation by August 1, 19___
  - ✔ Complete "dry run" presentation by September 21, 19___
  - ✔ Incorporate changes prompted by feedback from "dry run" by October 7, 19___
  - ✔ Complete second "dry run" by November 1, 19___
  - ✔ Send material for printing to printer by December 15, 19___
- By February 15, 19___ I have made my initial presentation to a pre-qualified audience of 25 people or more
  - ✔ Identify 15 target media for advertising by September 15, 19___
  - ✔ Prepare advertisement for target media by September 28, 19___
  - ✔ Buy Advertisments in 15 target media by November 1, 19___ in time to run by January 1, 19___
  - ✔ Contact 5 businesses each day to offer the presentation, starting on November 1, 19___
- By January 1, 19___ I am making 40 successful presentations a year and selling 24 widgets at each one
  - ✔ Develop a mailing list of 500 company prospects by December 31, 19___
  - ✔ Produce and mail my newsletter to 2,000 decision makers by June 1, 19___
  - ✔ Make 10 cold calls a day to pre-qualified prospects by June 31, 19___

(Sidebar 13A)

in one area than in others, and, if so, why? How can you use your strengths to achieve your goals and intentions in other areas? How can you redirect your energy from the more developed areas to the less developed ones?

Self-Knowledge is Personal Power

What does all this have to do with presentation skills? An effective presentatation is a projection of personal power. Not only does a presentation require clear intentions, but it also demands that the presenter have the self-trust and self-confidence to be credible. One of the best ways to develop all of these qualities is to keep your intentions in view and your accomplishments in mind. Defining your intentions makes them visible and brings them into your consciousness more emphatically. Listing your goals and your action steps makes you aware of your accomplishments and gives you valuable feedback about what you have done and what you are able to do. With this map in hand, your presentations will become focussed and succinct.

Self-knowledge opens the door to personal power, channels it, and makes it available. Self-knowledge is as simple as knowing you can do something and as complex as the mysterious power which allows us to reach out and touch others in profound ways. The source of personal power lies within ourselves. The way to find that source is to look for it and to cultivate it when we find it.

14

Seven Steps To Perfect Presentations

This chapter introduces a simple outline you can use to prepare for virtually any presentation. Every presentation can be build upon the answers to the seven questions in this outline. These answers will identify the information you need to know and become the building blocks of your presentation. How you present that information is entirely up to your judgment of what best suits your audience.

Seven Questions

(1) *What do you intend your audience to gain from your presentation?* Your first step, as always, is to clarify your intention. A clear understanding of your intention sends a message for action to your subconscious, which stimulates your intuition and guides your use of technical skills.

The more you know about your audience, the more specifically you can clarify your intention. It doesn't matter whether your audience is one or one hundred. For example, when a social worker studied Jane's home as part of her pre-adoption evaluation, Jane recognized that trust and emotional comfort were key concerns of the social worker. Accordingly, she focussed her intention: *Ms. White trusts us and feels comfortable in our home*. By clarifying her intention ahead of time, Jane was able to eliminate extraneous thoughts during the more stressful meeting.

Clarifying your intention is important even if you have to do it on the spur of the moment. If the phone rings and you find yourself facing a serious communication or if a casual conversation turns important, for example, put the other party on hold for a minute or take a short break so you can establish exactly what you intend to accomplish. If all else fails, excuse yourself from the conversation and call back in a little while when you are prepared.

Seemingly casual conversations between friends or loved ones require especially clear intentions. Even the most sensitive and thoughtful partners can go into 'automatic' at times, counting on history and intimacy to take the place of attention to each other's immediate needs. This often leads to indecision and stalemate. Whenever indecision and impasse appear, it's a signal that you need to clarify your intentions, because clear intentions give clear directions.

(2) What action do you want your audience to take? The energy of communcation must be turned into action for it to have value. The way to transform your thoughts, ideas, words, or message into action is to give commands for action to your audience.

Go back to your office and determine which of these recommendations you can implement.

Decide which of these seven ideas you can incorporate into your life.

On your way out the door, choose either the pink or the blue paper.

Implement one of these changes every day for the next thirty days.

Ask yourself what you can do right now to contribute to this goal.

Your goal is to motivate your audience to take action as a result of the energy of your presentation. *Inspire* your audience. Whatever action your audience takes will connect you and your message to them long after your presentation has ended. It will transform your speech from a fleeting moment to something with lasting value for the lives of the people you touch.

(3) What conclusion do you want your audience to reach as a result of your presentation? How would you like to be summarized? What one idea would you like to be foremost in your audience's minds and flow easily from their lips? The clearer a concluding image statement you create, the more likely your audience will be to remember it.

Trial attorneys have developed this skill to an art. Often, when preparing for a case, they look for a clear and memorable phase that sums up their case. They then use this phrase many times throughout the trial. The idea, which is often successfully implemented, is to create a clear image which the jurors will carry into the deliberation room and adopt as if it were their own.

A speaker usually has a limited amount of time in which to plant a lasting seed in people's minds. By taking the time necessary to develop a clear concluding statement, you can stretch the impact of your presentation for hours, days, weeks, or even years. Each time an audience member recalls the essence of your presentation, your message is given new life.

(4) What three headings sum up your presentation? Be able to summarize your presentation in three main ideas, or headings. Why three? Because three headings are easy for you and your audience to remember. Everyone can see the connection among the categories. Each heading supports the other two. And like a triangle, three is stable. If you think you have more than three main points, you need to simplify your thoughts. Stand back and look at your presentation from a distance. Ask yourself, *What are the really important points here?* List your ideas and look for common denominators among them. If you still have a rogue idea or two, ask why it doesn't fit into one of your three ideas. Rephrase it. If necessary, ask if it really is necessary to your presentation. Chances are, if you

can't work it into one of your three headings, it isn't. Eliminate it or build a separate presentation around it.

Give your entire presentation an organic integrity by making sure that each main idea helps your listeners understand the other two. An architect, for example, might develop a presentation that discusses general design considerations, the specific design considerations for a particular project, and the ways in which the project satisfies the general and the specific concerns. The same architect's presentation wouldn't work nearly as well if it discussed the merits of minimalist design, the advantages of low-volume toilets, and the aesthetics of adobe construction.

(5) Why is your presentation important to you? Why is it important to your audience? Your information is important to you. It is important to your audience. But not necessarily for the same reasons. You need to identify all the reasons. On the one hand, when you identify what is important to you, you can communicate your commitment. A given subject may not be the most important thing in your life in general, but it must be the most important thing at the time of your presentation. Let it affect you appropriately. Let your voice amplify the importance of the subject. The way you present your information will influence both the way your audience responds to your information and the way they think about the facts you have presented.

On the other hand, when you can discover what is important to your audience, you can reach out with a clear understanding of the similarities and differences between them and yourself. You can also begin building upon what you have in common. For instance, a politician may have legitimate political considerations that keep her from endorsing your ideas. Instead of ignoring their importance to her or questioning her integrity, you can acknowledge your difference of ideas and offer to find a way of satisfying both goals.

(6) What exactly is your viewpoint? A clearly defined statement of your viewpoint in your presentation opens a

window through which your audience can view your presentation. Your clear viewpoint enables your audience to see the ideas and concepts through your eyes. Invite the audience into your world by sharing your viewpoint.

This can be a challenge. It requires you to make a public commitment to your vision, and many of us feel vulnerable making this kind of public commitment. Nevertheless, it is not possible to persuade others without affirming your own personal commitment. Your viewpoint becomes a signpost for the audience. Many listeners will have come to your presentation with their own opinions. They will measure their viewpoints against yours. If you are vague or unclear about what you believe, your audience can only guess at your real message. Leaving results to chance makes things very unpredictable.

Let people know up front how you see your subject. If you see water conservation as a way of life, say so. If you consider meditation to be as important to you as breathing, say so. If you feel the long run is more important than the short run, say so. Don't leave the audience guessing. It can only foster misunderstanding.

This is just as important when you are representing a group, an organization, or a business. At these times, you need to express the viewpoint of the organization. Make sure you understand that viewpoint and why the organization sees the subject in that way. You cannot be effective unless you understand and can articulate the organization's viewpoint as clearly as you can your own.

(7) What is your real subject? This is not a redundant question. It is true that you have to understand your subject before you answer the first six questions. But you will discover that, as you analyze each question, you get deeper into your subject. Once you have completed your analysis, you may discover that your true subject is something other than what you first thought it was.

Suppose you, an expert in your field, have been asked to speak about a particular subject. If you do no more than list some thoughts and ideas and throw together some slides or graphics for good effect, you may never get around to your true subject, the reason you are presenting the information in the first place. Your audience may well walk away with a little additional information on a subject but not understand it any better than when they entered the room.

Just as you have learned to listen to the question behind the question, you need to look for the subject behind the subject. Finding this essence will allow you to address the point, issue, or idea that might otherwise stand between you and your audience. Take the time to consider and review your true subject. Your talk about global economics, for example, might actually be a plea for cultural understanding. Your talk about the company's new insurance plan might actually be a discussion about dealing with change. Only your understanding of the true subject can tell you what you really need to talk about. It is a cliché in business that you need to have a clear understanding of the business you are in if you hope to succeed. The same is true for a presentation. You need to have a clear understanding of what you are presenting.

The Block Becomes an Outline

When you are putting your presentation together, research your material more or less in the order of the seven steps above: intention; action; conclusion; the main ideas; importance to speaker and audience; your viewpoint; and your true subject. This general-to-specific passage of ideas helps focus your attention on the things that you need to establish.

When you outline your presentation, however, reverse the order of these elements: true subject; viewpoint; importance; main ideas; conclusion; action. This flow from general to specific helps you move your presentation to the action steps that you want your audience to take.

Leave your intention out of your outline. It may be the foundation on which you build your presentation, but a statement of your intention is not usually part of the presentation itself. Your intention is what you want to happen. Your intention will tell you what you need to say. Sharing your intention directly with your audience will not make your presentation a success; sharing it indirectly by carefully developing the parts of your presentation will. Don't share it; act on it.

Once you have developed the outline of your presentation, you can tailor it to suit the audience you are addressing. At times, for example, you may choose to elaborate on certain of the steps and deemphasize others or rearrange the order of presentation to meet the demands of a specific audience or presentation.Still, by developing your presentation along the outline of these seven steps, you will find that things come together naturally and smoothly.

Use this outline whether your presentation is a short introductory presentation or a lengthy seminar. For a brief presentation, your preparation will give you the skeleton you can draw from. For a more lengthy presentation on the same subject matter, all you have to do is flesh it out to include more information. Long or short, following this outline will give you the content you need, freeing you to concentrate during your actual presentation on applying your technical skills.

Let The Outline Fill Itself In

When you put your presentation together, let your subconscious participate in the process. Do some personal brainstorming. Allow your thoughts to flow freely around each of the building block areas. Take notes as you go over each step. Periodically review your thoughts. Even after you have completed all seven steps, go back to the beginning and play with the words and phrases that truly articulate your ideas. Read your words and phrases out loud, giving full attention to each ideas. As you practice you will continue finding more effective ways of phrasing your ideas. You will also find that your understanding of the words, phrases, and ideas is heightened with each review. With this will come an increasingly clear train of thought.

Once you have developed this train of thought (a *spine* in stage talk), trust yourself to know it. Keep your written presentation outline as simple as it needs to be—the building blocks in your chosen order and the main ideas you want to cover in two or three word phrases. That's all. It is easy to become so worried about detail that you try to write everything on the page. Paradoxically, however, the more detail you put on the page, the more confusing and distracting the page will become. To engage your audience, you must be free to speak directly to them, to see their eyes, to feel their thoughts, and to act on the feedback they give you. When you prepare properly for your presentation, all this worrying is unnecessary. Trust your preparation to guide you toward your presentation content and to send a clear message of your intention to your subconscious. Once your preparation is complete, you will be free to apply your energy toward the technical skills that will make your presentation come alive.

15

Preparing For An Interview

Television, radio, print, and personal interviews can be stressful. Knowing that what we say and how we say it is being scrutinized or recorded makes most of us self-conscious, and self-consciousness is the enemy of fluid communication. Where carefully selected words are a must, there is no room for self-consciousness.

Know Your Audience

Whatever your interview, it is essential that you know whom you are talking to. Research the interview just as thoroughly as you would research an audience for a sales presentation. Remember that interviewers are not there just to hear you speak. They will have their own agendas and reasons for speaking with you. The more you can find out about their goals, the better prepared you will be for the interview.

In a job interview, for example, learn all you can about the company and the position. What does this potential employer do? What kinds of benefits does it offer? What kind of commitment will it require from you? What kind of workplace atmosphere does it maintain? How many employees does it have and what is the typical longevity with the firm? Who will you be working with? What position will you be asked to fill? Only when you can answer these and similar questions can you make an informed decision about accepting the interview or the job. Once you feel that you want to be part of the organization, you can commit fully to acquiring the position.

If the interview is for the broadcast or print media, find out who the interviewer is. Does the person have a track record or an axe to grind? Is the interview likely to be friendly or antagonistic? Who is the audience? If the interview will appear on radio or television, will listeners be calling in? Will you be the only interview, or are you sharing the microphone with others? Answering these types of questions will help you sit coolly in the hot seat of media attention.

The Job Interview

Perhaps the most stressful interview is the job interview. You know that, by definition, your skill level and ability to complement the existing work force are being judged. It is not much easier for the interviewer, who knows that he or she has to make a decision that could have a profound impact on another person. For both, the interview can have significant personal results. The whole process can cause anxiety for everyone involved.

If you are about to be interviewed for a position, you need to prepare yourself in three general areas. You have to prepare your ideas, the specific information you want the interviewer to know about you. You have to take care of your personal appearance and your emotional state. And you need to prepare your materials, including your résumé, examples of your work, brochures, letters of recommendation, and anything else that documents your professional skills.

Before you begin your preparations, you have to know what you want. Several years ago I worked with Kaye, a woman who was so concerned about securing 'a position' that she never thought about securing 'the right position.' She was understandably concerned about things like the job market, the possibility that she would need to move outside the state, and her ability to command the salary she wanted. But she was so concerned about these outward trappings that she failed to ask what she wanted to do. In our very first session, she admitted that she was afraid she'd have to settle for a position she didn't really want. When I asked her to describe the type of position she did want, she couldn't. All she could talk about was the type of position she expected to get. She didn't know what she wanted, and that was about what she was going to get. Kaye had to recognize that she would never be a successful job hunter without a clear understanding of what success meant.

Once you have done your research and identified what you want, you can begin preparing for your interview by following the seven-step outline in Chapter 14. Begin by asking *What do I intend to achieve in this interview?* It's not enough to say *I want the job.* State an intention, one that involves the interviewer as well as the results of the interview. *The interviewer sees that my skills and experience answer the needs of the company* is much more useful and precise an outcome.

What actions will I ask my interviewer to take? Even as simple a request as asking for information can be a powerful part of your presentation. Suppose you are interviewing for a upper-level management position where you will be expected to complement or diversify the existing team. To demonstrate that you will make a good team member, ask questions that show your concern for the details of the operation, questions that show you have done enough homework to ask for information that only a member of the team could give you. *What are the inner workings of the organization? What is the president's attitude toward the work of the firm? What is the mission statement of the company and how is it implemented?* As you receive the information, notice how well your experience and beliefs mirror the goals and objectives of the company.

What conclusion must the interviewer reach about me and my abilities? Chances are, the interviewer already had made some positive judgments about you. Otherwise, you would not have been given this face-to-face opportunity. Your interviewer is comparing the impressions he or she got from your résumé to the impression you can make in person. Ideally, the conclusion your interviewer takes from your interview will support the promise of your paperwork and suggest that you are indeed the person the company is looking for. You already know what the company needs, so you have the opportunity to conduct your interview with an eye toward guiding the interviewer in that very direction.

Into what three areas can I group my experiences and ambitions? Recall that three main ideas or subheads is an ideal number. It is large enough to seem thorough and small enough to be manageable. This is just as true in a job interview. Three points are fairly easy for you to make and your interviewer to remember. More importantly, breaking your presentation into three well-defined areas forces you to spend the necessary amount of time looking at yourself and your career. This gives you an authoritativeness, a self-confidence, and a self-knowledge that can make you stand out as a candidate for the position. Whether you accept this particular job or not, the effect of developing this self-knowledge on your personal power and your career can be significant.

What is important to me? Do you want a home for your talents? Do you want an opportunity to develop your professional skills in a sympathetic atmosphere? Do you want the security of a large and well-established company with room to move up? Do you expect to make friends at work or only colleagues? Do you want a lifetime position or a stepping stone to later career advancement? Be clear about what is important to you.

What is important to the interviewing company? Is the company looking for a human resource who will contribute to the 'bottom line' or a human being who will strengthen the company family? Does the company expect a long-term commitment, or does it expect you to move on after a short time? Does the company expect you to help solve new challenges or only follow directions? Find out what is important before your interview. Confirm your findings during the interview.

What is my viewpoint about the position and the company? How do you think you can benefit the company? How do you see yourself fitting into the company and contributing to its mission? Ask your interviewer about the company's viewpoint. How does the employer see this position in terms of the company? How are you being viewed as a contributor to that role?

What is my real subject? What do you really want the interviewer to understand about you? What makes you and your background unique? What two or three word reminder can you develop to keep this element uppermost in your mind and in your interviewer's?

When Janet applied for a position with a health care provider, she knew that her ten years of experience in health and exercise gave her all the formal qualifications she needed. But she also anticipated—correctly, she later learned—that the structured company would be concerned that the professional freedom Janet was accustomed to might interfere with her ability to be a team player. Janet decided the true subject of her interview needed to be *partnership*. She kept the words "create a partnership" in her mind and used them several times during the interview. Janet got the job. Not coincidentally, she was given the freedom to run her department the way she felt it needed to be run within the parameters of the company's regulations. The "partnership" she spoke of proved to be a reward for both parties.

Preparing Yourself

Your personal appearance and your emotional state are as important in a job interview as they are during any other presentation. Your emotions support your mental preparation, and vice versa. If you have prepared well for your presentation, you should be confident in your ability to do the job. If self-confidence alone is not enough to dispell the tension of the job interview, review the techniques discussed in Chapter 8, "Turn Fear Into Excitement."

Your personal appearance is also important for what it communicates about you and your self-image. If you feel insecure about selecting appropriate clothing that looks good and suits the needs of your budget and your tastes, consider consulting a personal dresser. These consultants are free services in many fine department stores. Take advantage of the eyes of someone trained in the business.

In the theatre, this service is performed by the costumer. A costume designer has to make or obtain costumes that are appropriate for the period a play is set in, the social class the characters belong to, and the types of activities they are engaging in. At the same time, the costumer must be able to design clothes that fit the actors comfortably within the production's budget.

Use the costume designer's guidelines when you are picking out your clothes. Your clothing, including the colors, the style, and the fabric, all add to or detract from your impression. Be sure to consider all of these factors when you make decisions about your clothes. A garish madras jacket, for example, might not make the best impression if you are being interviewed by a conservative law firm. A well-tailored navy blue suit with a white blouse or shirt might be just the look that the firm is looking for.

Diane, a well-known and accomplished artist, came to our first appointment wearing a conservative silk dress. During this initial session, she told me about the artistic risks she has taken. The image she presented, however, was that of a middle-aged, conservative business woman. Why had she chosen that dress? She said it was what she thought people wanted to see. I suggested that she choose clothing that expressed her artistry while commu-

nicating her business sense. At our next meeting, she
wore a business suit and artistically complimentary acces-
sories. Not only did her new appearance reflect the artist
she was, but Diane also felt much more comfortable with
this honest image.

Prepare Your Materials

In the theatre, props are a character's personal effects. A
prop master makes sure that the character's props are appropriate for the character. Your props—the materials
you will present during an interview—should be appropriate for you. They should support the image you intend
to present. Even the colors you use, the paper you choose
for your letterhead, and the typeface you use on your cor-
respondence play important roles in your presentation.

Your material leaves an impression that goes far beyond what you say. Material that is sloppy or carelessly
designed says one thing about you. Material that is neat
and thoughtfully put together says something entirely different. Your material should leave a clear and honest impression of what you are like. If your props are well laid
out and easy to read and understand, they will support
the conclusion that you are organized, careful, depend-
able, and easy to work with. If they are flashy, colorful,
and ornate, they may leave the impression that you are artistic and flamboyant.

Your material is the only physical part of your presentation you can leave behind. Decide on the impression
you want your interviewer to have when all that is left as
a reminder is your material. How can your material support this impression? Take as much time as you need to
develop your props. The more authoritative their message, the more powerful your lasting impression.

The Interviewer's Perspective

The interviewee is not the only one making a presentation. An interview is just as much a presentation for the
person doing the interviewing. If you are the interviewer,
use the same seven-step process as you prepare to get past

first impressions and to look more closely at what the person you are interviewing has to offer.

Clarify your intention and that of your company. Beyond the job description, what qualities are important to you or your company? State the intention clearly. After the interview, review the intention and ask whether the person you just interviewed satisfied your intention.

Recognize the true subject of each interview. In all likelihood you will be interviewing a small number of candidates whose materials you have already reviewed. This will give you insight into the the true subject, those questions or concerns you want each candidate to clarify.

Identify your viewpoint ahead of time. During the interview, probe to understand the interviewee's viewpoint about the position. Listen to the words used and try to feel how sincere the interviewee is. Ask if the interviewee's viewpoint will support or undermine the position. A viewpoint is shaped by an attitude, so understanding an interviewee's viewpoint helps you understand the interviewee.

Be able to explain why the job is important to the company, and ask what is important to the interviewee. If your company cultivates a good corporate culture, for example, acknowledge that the employee-company relationship is important. Find out what the interviewee feels about working for a company in which interpersonal compatibility is important.

Identify three major ways the job relates to the central mission of your company. Explain these three ways to the interviewee and pay attention to the feedback you receive. This will tell you what interests and excites the applicant about the job and the company and where potential problems may lie.

During the course of the interview, you will make some preliminary conclusions about the interviewee. When you feel you have gained enough information, it is often useful to ask the interviewee to confirm or correct your impressions. In this way you give the potential employee the opportunity to strengthen her or his case or to correct assumptions, and you open the door to a frank, honest, and less formal dialogue. Asking the interviewee to take action on your conclusions adds clarity for you and gives the interviewee an opportunity to leave as complete an impression as possible.

Television and Radio Interviews

Preparing for a television or radio interview requires the same careful analysis. Know your intention, your subject, what is important to you, what is important to the listening audience, what your viewpoint is, the three main points of your subject, your conclusion, and the action you will ask your audience to take.

If you are interviewed live and you have to field questions from members of the listening audience, apply the techniques for finding the question behind the question. In a call-in interview where you are limited to hearing the voice of the caller, listen closely to vocal inflection, intensity, use of or lack of humor, use of pauses and, of course, the actual words. These will tell you as much as, and sometimes more than, the actual questions asked. Listen carefully, trusting yourself and your preparation to find the essence of the caller's question.

An interviewer may take on a viewpoint contrary to yours. An interviewer who seems to be on the same page as you can suddenly switch gears and oppose your basic idea. Interviewers try to speak for all segments of their audience. If an issue is sensitive or politically charged, for example, an interviewer may ask questions designed to lead you down an inappropriate or misleading path. If you find yourself facing an interviewer playing devil's advocate, acknowledge the problem—*I understand that many in your audience are concerned about this situation*. But don't let yourself be distracted—*However, it is a mistake to conclude that this project will contribute to that problem.*

The interviewer of a talk show has a separate agenda and will try to guide you along certain lines. This is both good and bad. It is good because it establishes a structure. The host is responsible for keeping the show moving forward; you are not responsible for that. On the other hand, the structure is established by someone else, someone who knows less about the subject than you do. The only way to counteract this effectively is to clarify exactly what you want to cover by stating your points even when you are not directly asked to. By all means, answer the questions you are asked, but then shift the discussion to bring up the points you feel are more important.

If the interviewer wants to establish a game plan before the show, take advantage of it. The interviewer may tell you the areas you will be questioned about. Knowing the types of questions you will be asked will help you find the angles for introducing your prepared material.

Always listen to what the interviewer is saying. Don't worry that listening will distract you from your message. Once you have prepared your thoughts and your materials, let go of your preparation and concentrate on the communication at hand. Listen to every word the interviewer says *as if for the first time*. Stay involved in the moment and respond to the here and now. Don't get flustered by a contrary interviewer. Make your responses as conversational as possible even if your interviewer is not playing by the same rules.

Stay focussed on your intention. This can be a challenge. Radio and television interviews that seem smooth and seamless to the audience are not always the same way behind the scenes. A good interviewer understands that drawing a guest into a mutual conversation can make for a much better show. And there are many good interviewers. But some interviewers always seem to do more than pay attention to their interviews, so be prepared..

When George was selected as the sole guest on a local talk show, he was ecstatic. His anticipation soared even higher when he discovered that he and the host shared a lot of common background. George arrived at the studio and received a list of subjects he and the host would talk about during the program. "How could this be better?" he thought. He went before the cameras, comfortable and confident...until the host asked his first question. "As soon as he was off camera and I was on, he started checking his microphone, looking at the monitor, and reviewing his notes. I was not prepared for this at all." George survived the experience because he had prepared well for the show and was able to speak to the image of the interviewer he had already formed in his mind.

Before The Camera

There are a few special rules for television appearances. Always relax, breathe, and focus on your information. Do not speak directly into the camera unless you are asked to do so—"making love to the camera" is difficult without substantial rehearsal and experience. Instead, let the camera capture you speaking naturally and comfortably to the person who is interviewing you or to studio audience members. Broaden your personal space. Remember that the camera sees everything. There are many potential disturbances in a recording studio. Develop your concentration and focus on presenting before the camera so you are not distracted by the many things that are going on in a television studio.

Meet The Press

A press or news interview is a fine opportunity to get your message out to many more people than your immediate audience. The trade-off is that your message is likely to be diluted. Most reporters will quote only part of what you say. That is why it is important to prepare as thoroughly for the press as you would for any other interview.

Use quotable phrases that leave little room for misinterpretation. Newspaper reporters are always looking to find a unique hook for the story. They also take themselves seriously. You may know your subject a lot better than they do, but even if you lay out the hook on a silver platter, make sure you acknowledge the reporter's ability to see it.

This is all the more important when you are interviewed for broadcast news. You can expect to see only about ten or twenty seconds of your interview during the broadcast, so put extra effort into coming up with quotable phrases—*news bites*—and providing the reporter with as much good material as possible. You may even increase your exposure if the amount and quality of the content is high.

A Final Word On Interviews

Whenever you are interviewed, remember that you are speaking, not just to the interviewer, but also to the company, the listening audience, the viewing public, or the readers of the publication. To address this broad audience, you have to be prepared. Know the issues surrounding your subject as well as you know yourself, and express yourself in succinct, precise, quotable statements. Prepare yourself well enough that, once you are in the interview, you can become completely involved in the moment and listen *as if for the first time*. Interviews do not have to become matters of life and death. Solid preparation and practiced techniques can make each interview a new and exciting experience.

16

Technical Concerns For Presentations

In theatre, the settings, lighting, and props create an atmosphere that helps the audience understand the play. Similiar design elements can add to the effectiveness of your presentations. Technical supports cannot do everything; they can only improve an already well-thought-out, researched, and rehearsed presentation. They cannot make up for a lack of vision or purpose. Well designed sets, lights, and props do not compensate for badly written scripts, poorly conceived shows, or badly prepared presentations. However, a well-developed and rehearsed production of any kind will be enhanced by well designed lighting, sound, and sets.

The Podium

Whether an individual speaker or a panel is presenting, a podium will generally be placed on the stage. Learn to use the podium effectively; its creative use can add to your presentation.

First, check the height. The podium should be low enough for everyone in the audience to see your head, neck, and chest, but it should be high enough for you to read your notes effortlessly. Never speak from behind a podium which is too large or too tall in proportion to your body. A correctly sized produm can increase your size and presence on stage. If the podium is too tall for you, ask that a step be provided. Otherwise, ask to have a different podium on stage. If you cannot get a podium replaced in time for your presentation, don't use it. Stand in front of it or beside it. Let your notes rest on it, but do not stand behind it.

The interplay of movement and immobility is an important dynamic in almost all presentations. Exposing your entire body to the audience makes for an open and honest impression. Use the podium as a home base and move away from it during your more expressive moments. Move back to the podium to explain technical information or support an intellectual or conservative image. If you find that the room is not conducive to movement, indicate movement by making slight shifts toward the side of the podium. Even this small movement, combined with a change in your attitude, can leave the desired impression.

When you use the podium as a set piece instead of the whole set, you increase your dramatic impact. Stand behind it, leave it completely, lean a hand on it in a casual conversational tone, pound your fist on it in real or mock demand. The more comfortable you become with using the podium as a tool, the more opportunity for variety and expression you will find.

Projected Visual Aids

Projections are the visual aids you use during your presentation. It is easy to expect too much from your projections. As graphic or colorful as they may be, they neither speak for themselves nor stand alone. Projections are supports for your presentation, nothing more. No matter how beautifully they are conceived, you cannot rely on projections to tell your story. You must tell your story and allow your visuals to illustrate your point.

Whether you choose slides, film, or overhead projections, make sure that the projected image is large enough to be seen easily and clearly by every member of your audience. If you require that your audience see certain details, make sure these details are visible from all parts of the room.

Whatever you project must be interesting to look at. The colors must be vivid, the lines distinct, and the designs clear and dynamic. Don't project any more than a single word or two. Lists and sentences of other kinds generally work better as hand-outs. (See the next chapter for some tips on handouts). If your audience is busy reading the screen, they aren't listening to you. A word or a short phrase, however, can be projected with great effect as long as you give the audience time to shift their attention. Pause for reading and reaction time, and remove the projection when it is time to move on.

Maintain a relationship with your projections. Use projections as if they were extensions of you. You selected your visual images because they depicted the idea you were describing. Join the audience in looking at them. If possible, stand near the image and use a pointer when you talk about aspects of the projection. If you cannot stand near your projection, gesture to it and look toward it as a cue that your audience should also look at it.

Use projections only if your subject will benefit by their inclusion. Don't use projections for the sake of using projections, and don't waste time on projections that are meaningless or distracting. If they don't help, don't include them.

If it is at all possible, practice with the equipment you will use. It can be disastrous for both you and your audience if you don't know how to operate a particular slide projector, if you can't see the image from the stage, or if you don't know how to focus images on the overhead projector. Make it part of your preparation to become comfortable with the projecting device you will use.

If you have an assistant operating your projections for you, be sure to practice with that person. Don't just assume that your signals will be recognized and followed. It is a blemish on your material, your audience, and your host if your presentation is ruined because of poorly conceived, developed, or executed projections.

Coordinate your visuals with your entire presentation. Poor coordination can lead to embarrassment, frustration, and anger. A world-famous architect known for his books, his buildings, and his artistry was once personally lecturing on his work. A ripple of anticipation and excitement surged through his audience. The presentation started out well. But at the end of his presentation, everyone went home disappointed. It all started when the architect stood between two projectors and asked his assistant to start the slide show. Neither projector was synchronized with the other or with the presentation. After a delay to synchronize the projectors, the architect resumed, now with his slides out of focus. In a short time, both the audience and the speaker lost patience, and everyone was unhappy well before the presentation was over.

Microphones

Know how to use a microphone, when to use it, and what kind of microphone to use. Hotel meeting rooms, for example, are generally equipped with a directional microphone attached to the podium. These pick up your voice only when you speak directly into them. If you plan to stand in one place for your entire presentation, a directional mike can be used with great effect. Likewise, if your presentation is outdoors, a directional microphone, which can eliminate the distracting sound of wind in the background, may be the appropriate choice.

If you will be speaking indoors and/or plan to move around, a stationary, directional microphone won't work. Here you will need a microphone you can carry with you and enough microphone cable to allow you to move at will. You may need help setting this up, so give yourself time before the presentation.

Speaking into a microphone requires skill. The technique is simple yet precise. Speak *over* the mike. Speakers who plant the microphone directly in front of their mouths obstruct their faces, look uncomfortable, and cause irritating, popping sounds by speaking too close and too directly into a mike. Speaking over the mike eliminates these problems. Once again, though, practice with the specific microphone you will be using. Each is different, and each requires its own special finesse.

Learn how to hold the microphone so that it is an extension of your hand. You need to find the ideal placement relative to your mouth and to synchronize your hand and your voice. When you increase your volume, move the mike a bit further from your mouth. When you drop your volume, move the microphone closer.

Many microphones are cordless. But if you will be using a corded model, you should practice handling the microphone cord with grace and ease. The cord will follow you wherever you go, so learn how to retrace your steps, moving the cord out of your way with an available hand or foot. In only a few hours of practice you can feel confident moving around attached to an umbilical microphone cord.

If you don't have the time or interest to develop this cord skill, you can use a lavaliere, a small microphone which attaches to your tie, jacket, or dress. This small but powerful microphone is paired with a battery pack that attaches to your belt or waistband. If you don't own one, ask that one be provided. Clip it approximately seven inches directly below your mouth on a piece of clothing. Make sure the microphone faces upward toward your mouth and that it does not rub against your clothing. The sound of anything touching it—a necklace, a scarf, your jacket, your hand in gesture—will be amplified. Speaking with a correctly placed lavaliere is a simple process. Your arms are free to gesture and you are free to move about the room with no concern for a cord.

Lighting

Just as a theatrical lighting designer helps to define the mood of the play, lighting can define the mood of your presentation. Meeting rooms are usually lit with general lighting that illuminates you and your audience with the same amount of light. This allows you to move to any part of the room and still be seen. But you receive no particular focus, even when you are standing at a podium.

A much more dramatic effect, often used in very formal presentations such as keynote addresses, is to spotlight the speaker. Two or more spotlights, from different directions, aim a narrow but very intense beam of light at the speaker while the lights on the audience remain relatively dim. The contrast makes for a strong theatrical image and focusses the audience's attention on the speaker. The intensity of the light, however, can make it difficult on the speaker. The experience of not being able to see your audience, for example, can be unnerving if you haven't been through it before. If you will be speaking under these conditions, by all means practice ahead of time with the actual lights.

A partially shaded speaker can be distracting and disturbing for the audience. When you walk into the room where you will be speaking, find out if additional lighting will be provided for you. If so, stand in it. Find the limits of the illumination on the floor and wall behind you. Experiment with how far you can move in all directions before you move out of your light. Look into the light to find the 'hot spot,' that part of the light which burns most brightly. By looking at the hot spot and once again moving in all directions, you can measure the practical limits of your movements. Once you find them, memorize these parameters and stay within them when you speak. As you get more comfortable with lights, a second clue is the temperature change that you feel as you move out of your light. The combination of area awareness and temperature sensitivity will allow you to stay illuminated. A speaker who knows how to use lighting to the best advantage has yet another tool to capture and keep the audiences' attention.

The lights will probably need to be lowered while you are using projections. Make sure there is a light at your speaking station. While the lights are low, you will also have less light illuminating you, reducing your range of movement. Differences in light affect your options. Practice in different lights, be aware of your parameters, and stay within your limits.

Technical aids can add visual and other support to your presentation. Once you become comfortable with the limitations imposed by lighting, microphones, the podium, and visual aids, you will find that you can use them to create an image that is bigger than life. For major presentations this image can be a dynamic tool. With careful preparation, you can use these technical aids, with all their limitations, as tools to create a complete and powerful presentation. Never overlook the usefulness of technical aids.

17

Major Presentations

Effective presentations before major audiences such as boards of directors must be clear, concise and accurate. They will be clear if you speak to the concerns of each audience member. They will be concise if you connect the issues effortlessly. They will be accurate if you prepare thoroughly and present your information with the assurance that thorough preparation makes possible.

These presentations may also be fairly technical. Professional organizations and boards of directors are busy, and they often meet for limited amounts of time. You won't always have the luxury of chatting or letting the presentation find its own direction. You may be called on to deliver nuts-and-bolts presentations that call for special kinds of preparation.

Know Your Audience And Your Stage

Before you begin your preparation, find out as much as you can about the concerns of the sponsoring organization, the audience members, the physical setting, and what you are expected to do. The more complex the issue, the more clearly you will need to understand these individual concerns so you can gear your information to address what each audience member wants or needs to hear. Because your audience is composed of decision-makers, the more directly you can speak to each one, the more impact your presentation will have.

Pre-Presentation Check List

Below are some specific questions to ask about your audience and the facilities. The information you gather will help you put together a presentation that satisfies everyones expectations.

1. The Audience.
• *What are the demographics of the audience? (size, age, race, professions, experience with the subject, education)*
• *What do you have in common with the audience?*
• *What objections are they likely to raise about your material?*
• *What will the audience gain from your presentation?*

2. The Speech itself.
• *What is the purpose of the meeting?*
• *What does the audience or the sponsor expect?*
• *Does the audience expect:*
  • *an uplifting or inspirational speech?*
  • *a formal or informal presentation?*
  • *a long or short speech?*

3. Technical and scheduling information.
• *What is the physical setup of the room?*
• *Will you need a microphone? Is a lavaliere available?*
• *How is the room lighted? How are the lights controlled?*
• *Is there a stage or platform?*
• *Is there a podium? If so, what size is it?*
• *Is the room air conditioned?*
• *What is the schedule of events?*
• *Are there other speakers? If so, where in the speaking order will you present?*
• *At what time of day will you speak?*
• *Who will introduce you?*

The Importance Of Handouts

It is often useful to leave clearly developed written materials in the hands of each listener in the audience. An effective handout will reinforce and/or extend the information in your presentation. It provides material that can be reviewed at a later date. If you are given too little time to discuss your subject effectively, a hand-out may become even more important as a means of getting your message into the audiences' hands.

Make sure your hand-out is compelling and highly readable. A hand-out on its own is rarely enough to make your case, but it can enlighten a well-thought-out presentation and make you much more persuasive. Spend the time to prepare first-rate handouts; design them with the same care as you design your presentation. Make sure they are clear and really do communicate what you want them to say. If your material is graphic—pictures or charts, for example—limit the words you use to headings or captions, or eliminate them altogether if that is appropriate. Choose your graphic material with an eye toward communicating your message clearly and readably while making the maximum impact on your audience.

Treat your hand-outs as if they were another form of visual aid. Keep them simple, designed to have a maximum visual impact with a minimum number of words. Give out one page at a time, and structure the presentation to allow time for your audience to absorb the printed information. Give only enough information to emphasize your point. Use different-colored paper for each page or idea. Try to see your hand-outs through the eyes of someone viewing them for the first time. Make your material as straightforward as you can to minimize the possibility of confusion.

At times, a 'one-inch handout' may be appropriate. This is a large package of material for individuals to look at later. During your presentation, recommend specific sections of the document for further reading; this makes a large handout seem less intimidating and increases the likelihood that your audience will follow through. Remember that you are trying to gain a favorable response from your audience. Whatever you do to make it easy for them to understand your position and act on your recommendations will bring your goal that much closer.

Putting Together A Major Presentation

It takes time to prepare an effective major presentation. Even if you have carefully followed the seven-step process recommended in Chapter 14, it often seems as if there just isn't enough time to prepare as fully as you would wish. The more time you allow, however, the more comfortable you will be with the final product.

Allow at least a week to complete the physical preparations, more if your presentation is sufficiently important. By allowing yourself a week or more, you can break your preparation into smaller, manageable parts, set a pace that you can commit to, and give your subconscious mind time to support your efforts. A week lets you eat the proverbial elephant one bite at a time.

Day One: Ask pre-presentation questions and begin brainstorming answers. One of the biggest mistakes a presenter can make is to become tied to a specific approach prematurely. This can turn a presentation of information that the audience needs to hear into a list of things the speaker has an itch to say. Take the time, on this first day of preparation, to find out who your audience is. Why are they interested in your subject? How does your subject affect their business? Only then can you begin to brainstorm effectively.

Brainstorming is a process of arriving at a solution or an answer. It involves listing every possible approach you can think of, even the ridiculous ones. Involve friends and colleagues in the brainstorming. The more minds you recruit, the more effective your brainstorming becomes. Let your mind just wander. The point is to open the door to every possible approach. Don't be critical. Simply list ideas and save the criticism for later, when you narrow your alternatives down. Don't commit to any approach at this time. If you lock yourself into an approach now, you can't give your subconscious a chance to help.

Day Two: Do your research, studying, and note-taking. No matter how well you know your material, digging a little deeper is always useful. What have others said about the subject? Your audience may have read some of this material, so knowing it is useful for you as well. If appropriate, also find out what others have argued *against* your concepts and ideas. You never know what is going to be useful in the end, so take notes about everything that seems remotely related. Often, material that you originally think is immaterial later proves to be helpful.

Day Three: Develop your seven building-blocks by defining your intention, your action, your conclusion, your body, your subject's importance, your viewpoint, and the essence of your presentation. After two days of feeding your subconscious, it is time to let your intuition and your hunches feed you back. If you need to, review Chapter 14, where building these blocks is discussed in detail.

This phase of preparation is important for any presentation, but it is especially crucial when you are preparing a major presentation. You need to know exactly what you will present, and why. Put it in writing. Let your earlier brainstorming and your research guide you toward succinct statements of each of your building blocks.

Day Four: Fleshing out your building blocks is the first step in putting your presentation together. Read the statements you wrote yesterday, making any corrections or additions you feel are necessary. Then brainstorm each statement. How are you going to communicate each building-block idea? Write down your ideas for each building block. Again, edit nothing at this time. Let your ideas and research flow out in writing under each heading.

While you are at it, brainstorm your handouts. Again, say *no* to nothing and do no editing. All ideas are valid at this point. Put them on the table for your conscious and your subconscious mind to play with.

Day Five: Begin giving shape to your presentation. Take a few minutes to focus your attention, then review your brainstormed ideas from yesterday. With a pen or a highlighter, identify those word or phrases that best capture the essence of your thoughts. If necessary, change a word or two to clarify what you mean, but don't get bogged down in fine-tuning. The important thing is to find the words and phrases that best capture your meaning in terms your audience will understand. If you can't find enough material to summarize your intent, you may need to redo the brainstorming activities of yesterday.

Once you have isolated the really meaningful phrases, look for the connections between and among your ideas. How does one building block connect to the next? How do your ideas connect to each other? What are the central themes? Explore these interconnections until you have found the threads that hold the entire presentation together.

Then, test the linkages by speaking your ideas out loud. Explain each section casually and conversationally. Go over its important points and how it contributes to the whole package. Speak to yourself if you have to, or speak to a friend and ask for feedback.

Day Six: You are now ready to put your presentation into outline form. By this time, you should be able to see your subject and your entire presentation clearly in your mind. Your outline will result from the clarity with which you can see both the big picture and the details. You need to be clear about your aims if you want to make a useful outline.

Keep your outline simple; I like to limit mine to one- or two-word reminders for each of my building blocks. If you have done your preparation well, you won't need much more than this to deliver your presentation. Don't write down so much that you end up consulting your outline every few moments; nothing can kill the spontaneity of an otherwise good presentation more quickly. Arrange your thoughts in the order you plan to give them; jot down when and where to give out handouts or show overhead projections; and trust your preparation and knowledge to do the rest.

Start putting your handouts and visual aids together. These need to be prepared ahead of time, so you will either need to produce them yourself or send them out to a printer or a service bureau. Either way, you will need to have them in your hands when you march into the room to make your presentation.

Day Seven: This is dress-rehearsal day. Go through each step of your presentation as if you were actually delivering it. Create a realistic environment for your rehearsal—one that resembles the room where you will be presenting as closely as possible. If you will be using electronic aids, have them ready to work with. If you will be using a podium, practice with a table or box of appropriate height. If you can, have a tape recorder or a video camera ready to record your rehearsal. Using your outline, go through your presentation section by section and building block by building block. Take notes and, if possible, get feedback from a friend or a colleague. Then rehearse again as often as you need to get your presentation down pat.

Throughout the stages of preparation, don't neglect your vocal and physical exercises. From the first day to the last, continue working on those skills that improve your ability to deliver your content. Preparing yourself physically, vocally, and mentally is just as important as preparing your material. Allow these exercises to support your preparation. Don't wait until just before your presentation to begin. It won't help nearly as much as making yourself ready well beforehand.

Presentation Day

By the time you finally deliver your major presentation, you should be fully prepared. Start the day feeling like a professional presenter who has taken control of the presentation. Begin by completing your vocal and physical warm-up and mastering your voice and body. Make sure that all your materials are where they need to be and that your equipment is working properly. Review your message so that you are in charge of what you are saying.

Know your environment. If you can, practice in the room where you will be working. Stand at the podium well before your presentation. Like the actor who walks the stage before a performance, check your props and feel as if you have control over the space. (This is such a common practice in the theatre that stage managers routinely give 'time calls' to actors to let them know how long they have until the audience is allowed to enter the building.) Do as the professional performer does and take possession of the presentation room. Look around the space and tell yourself, "This is my room; I own this space; I am in control."

Preparation has to come before presentation. You cannot do both at the same time (though some people always seem to try). Don't kid yourself that spontaneity and casual style are the results of off-the-cuff speaking. And don't insult your audience by making a poorly thought-out presentation. What makes for respectful, spontaneous, casual, off-the-cuff, persuasive speaking is the firm grasp of the subject and the practiced technique that come from solid preparation.

Your audience will receive your presentation much more openly and you will enjoy the process much more fully if you prepare effectively. Adapt the pace of your preparation to your own needs and schedule. Whether you complete the process in seven days or whether you complete it over a period of several weeks is not important. What matters is that preparation works, but only if you do it.

18

Presentation in Everyday Life

Presentation skills are part of a broader collection of communication skills. When you present, you are representing yourself to the outside world. It would be nice if all you had to do to make your points effectively was to follow the instructions in this book. But communication flows in two directions, not just one. It is, in reality, a give-and-take interchange involving tasks as diverse as problem-solving, cooperating, and bringing order out of chaos.

Your presentation is your contribution to a dialogue. A good presentation can help achieve your communication goals. But you cannot take for granted that others are going to be receptive or open to what you are saying. The presentation of yourself always takes place in the context of a not-always-willing audience.

All communication is important, even the seemingly small communications that take up most of our days. These may be small encounters that are easy to take for granted, but they follow the patterns we have internalized for our more self-conscious dealings. These day-to-day mini-communications are rehearsals for the larger, seemingly more important ones that we put so much of our energy into.

Presentation skills can make everyday communications smoother. This last chapter is intended to bring presentation back to the real world. It offers several theatrical and presentation techniques you can use to clarify your intention and awareness even when the circumstances seem unimportant or insignificant.

Who...What...Where

If they hope to create a convincing performance, actors must identify the *who, what* and *where* of the situation. *Who* is the character in the situation? *What* is the character trying to accomplish? *Where* is the action taking place? By focusing on the answers to these questions, actors can alter their presentation styles to meet the communication needs of the immediate situation.

Patty and Louis have learned to apply this technique in the kitchen. Both of them love to cook, though each of them cooks in a different way. After a few fights and several memorable demonstrations that too many cooks do, indeed, collapse the soufflé, they learned that *who, what,* and *where* were very practical concepts. They began playing a kitchen game called "Master and Servant" in which they had to define *who, what,* and *where* before they even started.

One of them becomes the master of the recipe; the other becomes the servant. Whoever is the 'master' is in charge, and whoever is the 'servant' follows the master's directions exactly. The master is responsible for making sure that everything works, that all the ingredients are available and at hand, that the recipe is followed in the correct order. The servant simply follows instructions without embellishing them or adding any personal touches. After only a short time of acting as master and servant, Patty and Louis discovered the role-playing worked. They became so adept at playing their roles that they were able to be both master and servant simultaneously.

SMEAC

A second technique borrows heavily from the military communication model, SMEAC. This unattractive-sounding acronym, short for *Situation, Mission, Execution, Administration,* and *Command,* describes a useful communication method which analyzes situations in terms of their dynamics. *Situation* calls for understanding the context in which the task or the communication is to be accomplished. *Mission* involves stating the task precisely. *Execution* requires the exact definition of how the task will be performed. *Administration* spells out the logistics, the supplies and equipment which will be needed to complete the job. And *communication* describes who is in charge and how questions will be answered and information exchanged.

Todd used the SMEAC model when he and a small crew of workers built the stairs for one of our plays. He defined the situation: "Here is the stage; here is where the stairs go; I am in charge; Joe is my assistant; Fred, Tom, and Korey do the dirty work." Then he stated the mission: "We are going to build the stair unit for Act II; it will go from this point to that point." He spelled out how the task would be executed: "Fred, Tom, and Korey will cut the wood to the proper lengths, which I have marked out; Joe will nail the boards together." He specified the logistics: "Put on protective glasses and use the table saw to cut the boards; then hammer the boards together with the power hammer which is in the tool cabinet." Finally, he clarified the command: "If you need to speak with me or if there are any problems, I'll be in the office ordering more materials; just walk in."

What Is Going On Here?

It is an unhappy fact that many people put much less energy into their presentation and communication than you put into yours. This doesn't mean that you have to resign yourself to living in a world of misunderstanding. *Who...What...Where* and SMEAC are techniques that you can use to read between the lines of any communication, whether large or small. They are effective when you are in charge. And they are particularly useful when you are not in charge and you need to understand what is going on.

If you find yourself in a confusing or unsatisfying communication, for example, stand back and ask a few basic questions. *Who* is in control here? *What* is going on...or supposed to be going on? *Where* is this supposed to be taking place? Then use the SMEAC model to analyze the situation and answer questions as if you were the one in charge.

When Maria found herself working with a very uncommunicative contractor, she used the techniques to help her complete some aggravating communications. This contractor was expected to repair the office air conditioning. It was supposed to be done during evenings and weekends so as not to disrupt business any more than necessary. Her analysis of the situation raised questions that had to be answered: *Are you responsible for doing the work within your estimated cost and time-frame? Who will do the actual work? What are the terms of your warranty?*

She then questioned the mission: *What do you propose doing? How do you know that it is going to work?* How would the job be executed? *How will you proceed with the work? How long will it take? How long will we be without air conditioning?* And what about the administration? *What materials will you be using? Will you be providing those materials or will we? How many workers will you be using? What will you need from us?* Finally, how would the command work? *Where will you be while the work is being done? How will we be able to communicate with you if we need to?*

Maria used these techniques to help her understand a difficult but important communication. They work equally well to make ordinary and routine communications run smoothly. I know people who have even used these techniques to plan a surprise party—very successfully I should add.

Seven Building Blocks Revisited

The same seven building blocks that you use to develop your presentations can also help you in everyday communications. Whether you are dealing with an institution or a single individual, always begin by understanding your intention. How do you want this interaction to turn out? What is your viewpoint on the subject? How do you really feel about the issues involved? How important is this to you? How important is it for the party you are dealing with? What kind of conclusion should your communication partner leave the encounter with? What actions do you want to see taken as a result of the exchange? What conclusion do you want the communication to reach?

Examine these questions until you are satisfied with your answers. It is often said that "if you don't know where you are going, that is exactly where you will end up." This is just as true for communications. The clearer you are about each part of the interchange, the better able you are to arrange an outcome that satisfies everyone. The more unfocussed you are, the more the interchange drifts and the less influence you have over the outcome.

Presentation And Life

Life is not a bed of roses, and even if it were, no amount of communication or presentation skills could strip the thorns from the stems. Sometimes, despite your best efforts, you will run into conflict. This is not necessarily the fault of bad communication techniques. Some of the people you meet simply thrive on conflict—whether their reasons are constructive or destructive you may never be able to tell.

That does not mean you should shrug your shoulders and give up your attempts to communicate clearly. You are not responsible when someone else refuses to listen. Fortunately, for every person who seeks out conflict, there are many people who truly do want to hear what you have to say.

Effective presentation skills and effective communication skills are parts of the same challenge—the challenge of making your way through a world you have to share with others. What makes this such an exciting challenge is that you *can* rise to each occasion, even when you are bewildered by doubts. Not everyone will rise, but those of you who do will find an electrifying, standing-room-only world where you are in control of your own destinies.

The presentation skills discussed here will help you become successful in all your social interactions. The first step is to decide your vision, to know why you are involved and what you want to achieve. Acknowledge your intention, listen to your intuition, and hone your technique. Become the person you want to be.

Other Books from
Silvercat Publications

The Travel Health Clinic Pocket Guide To Healthy Travel
by Lawrence Bryson (ISBN 0-9624945-4-2, $13.95)
*Guidelines for traveling safely and staying healthy on the road
by the medical director of San Francisco's Travel Health Clinic.*

Moving: A Complete Checklist and Guide for Relocation
by Karen G. Adams (ISBN 0-9624945-6-9, $8.95)
Checklists, tips, and ideas from a veteran of 30 moves.

How To Be Smart Parents Now That Your Kids Are Adults
by Sylvia Auerbach (ISBN 0-9624945-8-5, $14.95)
*A wise, practical guide to the rewards and challenges
of being parents to grown children.*